Advance Praise

. . . . . .

"At once powerful and thoughtful, Kaplan and Manchester have created an inspirational guide to help leaders get the most out of their teams. This book will change your business—and your life!"

—MARSHALL GOLDSMITH, author of #1 *New York Times* bestseller *Triggers: Creating Behavior that Lasts—Becoming the Person You Want to Be*

"*The Power of Vulnerability* shows how you can fully embrace your authentic purpose to bring passion to your work and to guide others to do this, too. This easy to read and practical guide is a must for everyone on your team."

—PAUL J. ZAK, author of *Trust Factor: The Science of Creating High-Performance Companies*

"Too often, leaders believe that success comes from their ability to wear 'many different hats.' *The Power of Vulnerability* dashes that myth. Top leaders know how to live authentically, operating from a place of passion and openness. Kaplan and Manchester tell leaders how to look inward as a way to build stronger, more satisfying relationships. Immature leaders strive to create followers; vulnerable leaders know how to create a team of leaders."

—SCOTT CARBONARA, author of *Manager's Guide to Employee Engagement* and *Go Positive! Lead to Engage*

"*The Power of Vulnerability* fundamentally changes how leaders think about relationships in their business. It's a smart innovative shift in thinking and approach that can transform the culture of your team and organization."

—DAVID LANDSBERG, president & CEO of Goodwill Industries of South Florida, former publisher of the *Miami Herald*

"*Power of Vulnerability* is well written with valuable insight for leaders interested in building positive, strong relationships, and better team performance. Highly recommend!"

—**WILLIAM SIDER**, former CFO of Hertz Rental Car

"Shift180 has brought the principles of *The Power of Vulnerability* to me and my companies. They have been a force in my life! Shift180's coaching and systems around every major part of my life have moved me forward to remarkable success. I doubled my income, was promoted to CEO, tripled the revenue of my company, and lost over 100 pounds as a direct result of their work. They unleashed power in me I didn't know I had. Even when I wasn't the most open to coaching, they empowered through to help me get over myself and continue to succeed. I thank God every day for placing Shift180 in my path."

—**MARCIA BARNES**, CEO of Valve + Meter; 2012 Woman
of Influence *Indianapolis Business Journal*

THE
POWER
OF
VULNERABILITY

THE
POWER
OF
VULNERABILITY

HOW TO CREATE A TEAM OF LEADERS
BY SHIFTING INWARD

· · · · · ·

BARRY KAPLAN

AND

JEFF MANCHESTER

GREENLEAF
BOOK GROUP PRESS

This publication is designed to provide accurate and authoritative information in regard to the subject matter covered. It is sold with the understanding that the publisher and author are not engaged in rendering legal, accounting, or other professional services. If legal advice or other expert assistance is required, the services of a competent professional should be sought.

Published by Greenleaf Book Group Press
Austin, Texas
www.gbgpress.com

Distributed by Greenleaf Book Group

For ordering information or special discounts for bulk purchases, please contact Greenleaf Book Group at PO Box 91869, Austin, TX 78709, 512.891.6100.

Design and composition by Greenleaf Book Group and Kim Lance
Cover design by Greenleaf Book Group and Kim Lance
Image credit: ©pialhovik/istock/Thinkstock.com

Cataloging-in-Publication data is available.

Print ISBN: 978-1-62634-473-0

eBook ISBN: 978-1-62634-474-7

Part of the Tree Neutral® program, which offsets the number of trees consumed in the production and printing of this book by taking proactive steps, such as planting trees in direct proportion to the number of trees used: www.treeneutral.com

TreeNeutral

Printed in the United States of America on acid-free paper

18 19 20 21 22 23   10 9 8 7 6 5 4 3 2 1

First Edition

To our children, Chris, Allie, and CJ.

CONTENTS

• • • • • •

CHAPTER 1

The Journey Begins: Isn't It Time?

· · · · · ·

We Want More

WE ALL WANT the same thing. More. Even though we come from different places and diverse backgrounds, most of us yearn for something that we do not yet have. Or, at least, we think we don't have it or even know how to describe what might be missing.

Do you want more? Do you feel like you are going through the motions at work? Are you struggling to find meaning in what you do? Are you resigned to your current role by saying this is all there is? Are you disengaged from your colleagues and feel as though there isn't a true sense that you are all a team? In some senses, does it feel like you are dying a death of 1,000 paper cuts, feeling like you care a little less with each passing day?

If you have felt or currently feel this way, you are not alone. Many of the business leaders and professionals we work with tell us they have a sense of feeling alone. And, we've also experienced this yearning with artists and politicians, clergy and students, and among dreamers and pragmatic collaborators.

So how do you shift from that sense of feeling alone or disengaged into a sense of connection? How do you shift from feeling like a drone completing your work into feeling inspired by being a part of and aligned with something that has a sense of purpose?

Our book's title, *The Power of Vulnerability: How to Create a Team of Leaders by Shifting INward*, speaks to a concept that we call "INpowerment." Not to be confused with empowerment, INpowerment comes from our beliefs that:

- each individual and team have more power than we realize,

- each of us has the capacity to access the power inside us,

- we can learn how to do it,

- we can do it on our own, but even better as a team, and

- we need to discover and unleash that power by shifting inward.

The potential of INpowerment reaches beyond our imaginations, yet it requires the courage of vulnerability to join the journey.

To help break the ice working with groups and teams, we invite participants to stand in a circle and take a step forward if they identify with one of over forty statements we read. We'll ask them to step forward "if you have a post-graduate degree" or "if you played on a high school sports team"—as part of a warm up round, and then gradually we offer more intimate statements.

When we say, "Step in if you believe you are not using all of your talents in your current role," almost everyone takes a step in. Each of them believes they are limited in what they can offer and contribute to their team. There is a palpable gap between the individual's perception of their output and their potential; and each time we conduct this exercise, we can feel the tension and possibilities at both the individual and team levels. Not only is the individual living in a "less than" state, but the team is achieving less than it could if the members were organized so that each person was able to access more potential talent and put it to use.

The good news is that these people actually believe they have innate and learned talent. The bad news is that they're not using it. Often they've given up the *belief* that they have the power to use all of their talents. Or they have given their power away.

We can explore how to maximize your power at the individual level and the team level—a process we'll engage in throughout the book.

Individually, each person who steps in during these exercises is yearning to be seen for their potential and pleading to contribute more.

At the team level, the individuals want to be part of something bigger than they are—a team or organization where they will be counted on and can count on others to contribute to its success. They want what they don't have: more. They know that their success depends not only on their improvement but also on their cooperation with others.

All of these folks want to join the journey.

Disconnected from the Source

So why are these leaders from different backgrounds feeling this way? Where can they find the *more* that they're searching for? What do they have in common?

They are all people who feel disconnected from their purpose and authenticity, and who feel alone or uninspired by others on their team.

They show up for work just to go through the motions and get through the day. While they cooperate with others as appropriate and necessary, their objective is simply to complete the task, usually without regard for a grander individual or team purpose.

All of this disengagement creates a huge sense of "aloneness" in the workforce. Our disconnection from purpose and authenticity is the root cause of this loneliness and lack of inspiration.

These people are lonely. They are members of lonely teams. And when they speak about this challenge, it is usually to complain about it. It is lonely at the top, the middle, and the bottom. At all levels of the organization, people feel disconnected and without power. They get the work done with mind and body, yet still yearn to have a natural and soulful connection to others. So, not only are they holding back from contributing their true value to their team, they neither give inspiration to nor receive it from others. And this aloneness is contagious.

These lonely individuals and teams are disconnected. There is a lack of enthusiasm, and the day takes forever to pass by. The "more" they seek is connection. But from what are they disconnected? To what or whom do they need to connect? What is keeping them from fulfilling these connections?

We believe they are disconnected from their source—their purpose and authenticity. This source can only start with the individual. It's the feeling when you get out of bed in the morning—sometimes even before the alarm goes off—when you cannot wait to seize the day because you are deeply engaged at a level that is awe-inspiring yet indescribable. A person's source is a unique imprint. And, because it is indescribable and unique, those who have never experienced it have a difficult time understanding what it means.

Purpose is the reason why we are here, the connection to the cause—small or large; it just feels right and makes sense. Authenticity is the quality of being real. When the two intersect, there is an emotional connection with intense enthusiasm when time seems to pass by without notice.

When you do not know why you're doing something, or don't have any emotional connection to it, you will likely feel lonely. And when you feel lonely, you are unlikely to engage with others enthusiastically. So, the malaise that you bring to the team will pull the others down rather than lift them up. The good news is that the same logic works in reverse toward a positive outcome.

You have undoubtedly felt, during certain times in your life, a clear sense of purpose or direction. When you are connected to yourself and feel that internal source of inspiration, the days fly by! You are happy, excited, and fulfilled. You may feel a deeper sense of connectedness to your teammates, as they share in the broader vision. Being aligned, working together toward a greater purpose, and being committed to making a vision reality can be one of the most fulfilling aspects of our careers.

So, the journey from loneliness to connection starts with the awareness that something is missing, and a desire to explore purpose and authentic connection. As an individual, you want to get clarity about your purpose or cause, to choose and embrace your "why" before you take on your to-do list, and to know that it is right when you are being real.

A team's source of power lies with members connecting first to their own purpose and authenticity. If all members show up disconnected, the team will be nothing more than a bunch of lonely souls. Yet when each person has clarity and is aligned with their purpose, it will be a connected—and powerful—team.

Creating a shared vision and deeper connection within a team or department takes time. It's an investment. In a culture that wants a quick ROI, many times the time invested into our human capital and relationships doesn't provide an immediate, quantifiable impact to the bottom line. In many organizations, that process is allocated to an annual offsite, where the organization can have two days filled with *kumbaya* moments, and then get back to work.

Who Unplugged Us?

Why, in our interconnected world of ubiquitous communication, are we disconnected from others and ourselves? How did this happen? What is our responsibility in creating our purpose?

Our culture thrives on what is convenient, easy, and quick. This is what we call a master overlay for our culture. This culture pretends to keep us totally connected with everyone all of the time. While we are tethered to multiple devices that ostensibly connect us, we have become untethered from our inner souls and those who matter most to us. Instead of high-quality, low-quantity synchronous touch—like walking into someone's office and talking—we have migrated to low-quality, high-quantity asynchronous touch—such as sending an electronic message to the person sitting next to you. Lines of banal texting with emoticons have replaced looking into someone's eyes and feeling a soulful connection. We have replaced going to a theatre, watching a film together, laughing, crying, or clapping in catharsis as a group with asynchronous, individual viewing or binge-watching entertainment on personal devices. As an unintended consequence of technology, we have stripped ourselves from our humanity. Instead of looking inside for our purpose, we are now trained to look down at the device of the day for a script.

External solutions—online and offline—abound for every challenge. Sitting around a table in discussion about a banal factoid, we all turn to our phones and quickly search for the answer. We have hyperlinked ourselves to what we're convinced is a higher knowledge platform, and yet in the process we have disconnected from the ultimate source of wisdom that resides INside.

It is so much easier to blame or look to others for problems and solutions. And in our world today, sponsors of fast-track solutions are targeting us in hot pursuit, no matter where we click or turn. Our culture is at the point where we are unconsciously seduced by constantly streaming offers. Even when we refuse one, another more tempting one appears on our screens. As a result, we tend to shut down and check out, resulting in a loss of "you" as a source of inspiration and wisdom.

It's not surprising that our internal connections have been hijacked. It is tough work to even think about, let alone work on, "purpose"—and the whole notion of being "authentic" poses a grave risk. What if our real selves turn out to disappoint others or ourselves? And the purveyors of so-called solutions for everything I need (and don't need) know our weaknesses. Try doing a search for "how to connect to your purpose" or "ten steps to becoming authentic." You'll discover no shortage of surefire suggestions that commoditize and commercialize a journey that should be unique to you. As you'll see, purpose is not some esoteric dream, but a deep connection to the core of what's important to you, today, NOW.

If our real power comes from connecting to the purpose and authenticity that are unique to each of us, then the road to connecting with others on our teams will have to start with ourselves. Unfortunately, cultural biases are working against us.

Technology Quicksand

Imagine you're going on vacation and want to take advantage of staying connected to your office, friends, and family. Even though you click "out-of-office assistant" on your email settings, you still check messages every time you have an Internet connection. And, each time you sneak a peek, you end up moving away from where you are and into the place you are supposed to be away from. Each time you check your messages, you are stepping in technology quicksand.

We don't need to travel far to find quicksand—it's even in the office. It's waiting to invite you in to a one-way-only detour, even as you're seated side-by-side with your colleagues at the conference table. As the projector broadcasts a bunch of graphs on the big screen, you lose your focus for a moment when you sense a vibration in your pocket—a sign that you can be removed from the formality of the presentation (well, you could always access it later on the shared drive) and instead be drawn to a beacon (your phone) that could be a more important opportunity, or at least more enticing than what's on the big screen. And, there you go, into the void of someplace other than where you are supposed to be right here and now—disconnected from purpose and people, alone even in a crowded room.

Quicksand sucks in anything falling into it and is hard to escape from. It attracts us through the lure of taking on more devices, tools, and ways to stay in touch with business, family, friends, and the world. We even take the connection to the bathroom, learning from an early age how to multi-task multiple things all of the time. Continually captivated by the myriad possibilities of connecting to the most information and most people, we can no longer escape from the servitude of technology quicksand.

Starting with a noble intention, we end up defeating the intended goal—we move further away from meaningful connection rather than closer. The volume is too high, too loud. There are hundreds of channels, but we are tuned out to what matters most and to who we are really meant to be—our authentic purpose.

And, all hooked up amid lots of noise, we are alone, unfulfilled. Disconnected.

Tripping over Myself and Going Nowhere

This lack of connection gets us stuck.

**What keeps us stuck in the same place
are our self-limiting beliefs.**

We create limits for ourselves and we actually spend energy finding ways for these boundaries to be reinforced by others. Ultimately, they become embedded into our internal operating system of how we must show up in our roles and perform our jobs.

These limiting thoughts include:

- Beliefs about how much of ourselves we can reveal in meetings

- Beliefs about our roles in the leadership of a team, department, or organization without being the hierarchical boss

- Beliefs about the appropriateness of more real, open, even vulnerable conversations

- Beliefs about our ability to take risks within the organization

- Beliefs about our own powers, authority, and/or ability to change our circumstances

- Beliefs about the combined capabilities of the team.

- Beliefs about our ability to feel a deep sense of fulfillment

- Beliefs in our and the team's ability to handle chaos

If we subscribe to this way of thinking, we may believe "I am who I am because my business card says so. This never happens to someone in my position. It's never been done that way before. It's always been done this way. So it always is that way." And so on.

Management practices have long been founded on hierarchy and order. There is a structure to how decisions are made. Countries work this way. Institutions work this way. Families work this way. Without hierarchy, there would be anarchy, so organizations certainly work that way.

In an organization, if you are not in a high-level box on the organization chart, then you are a follower, not a boss or leader. Additionally, in the past, there never has been a place for emotions or personal issues in the workplace. They have been, frankly, unacceptable. We are all expected to keep a stiff upper lip, show no emotions, and keep our cards close to the vest. We are, in many ways, asked to be good little robots, emotionless, tireless—and just get the job done. The less drama, the better, we are told.

We grow up in a world where identity forms early, shaped by the home and community in which we grow up, influenced—directly and indirectly—by parents, family, teachers, and other elders. Often though, unintentionally, we more easily absorb and start to take on the belief that we will live a life within clear and preset boundaries. And our power is, therefore, limited by those bounds, and our self-limiting beliefs are born from these demarcation lines—ceilings that govern how far we can reach up based on how the outside world has set us up for life. Then, these self-limiting beliefs become self-fulfilling prophecies and we get our jobs done only as we are instructed. We stay on the job with others, much like us, who suffer from similar self-limiting beliefs, and side-by-side yet very much alone and lonely, we work until quitting time and come home without hope that the next day will bring a better outcome.

There is a switch on this story line, however.

These self-limiting beliefs are self-fulfilling—unless we choose to change the belief. (Now that's hard to swallow, since one of the most common self-limiting beliefs is that we can't change belief systems.) At some point we can become aware that we are tripping over ourselves, or that our self-limiting beliefs about our power and potential are causing us to remain stuck in place. That if we take ownership for tripping ourselves, then we can no longer blame others for our situations. Now we are free to take responsibility for moving forward through changing our belief systems. Instead of finding how much power we have given to us from those on the outside, we can look inside for the answers of where our power is, where we belong, and what we want.

Think of it as though you and your team are running a DOS 1.0 operating system. Think you might need an upgrade? This is the journey!

We must look at our internal operating systems and find new ways to INpower ourselves and our teams so that we can break through and create a new upgrade—a way of doing business that will leverage and maximize the internal power of our people.

CHAPTER 2

For Return to Connection: INpowerment Is Worth It

· · · · · ·

No Way Out but Change

CHANGE HAPPENS WHEN the pain of suffering is just too great to endure the status quo, when inertia gives up to the pressure point of desperation. Few enjoy change, yet the choice is: change or lose your employees and ultimately your market value. Your employees and team members will serve as the catalyst for change and vote with their hearts, minds, and then their feet—unless and until leadership comes from the heart of the organization.

The first sign of a need to change comes when employees disengage—they check out emotionally while still showing up for work on time and doing their jobs. When a work environment discourages you to show up and work through your emotions, you'll check your feelings at the door. The emotional disconnect is a defensive reaction to discontent. It comes from a feeling that you are better off being numb rather than connecting to your real feelings of sadness, anger, frustration, and hopelessness. You will numb yourself to avoid or deny your sadness and frustration as a coping mechanism to get through the day. However, you are actually pretending to quash your negative emotions (because they'll inevitably emerge in some unintended, sideways fashion), and you also close the opportunity to connect with others with empathy so you miss out on deepening relationships.

Next comes the employees' intellectual or mental disconnect while still working with the organization. If you reach this stage, you'll use your smarts to game the system and find a way to look for a better job while staying on payroll. You and your coworkers sit at your desks, turn in timely reports, with a goal of keeping your jobs (or not being fired or found out), buying time to the next bonus pay-out—yet your creativity, ingenuity, and thirst for growth is gone. Whatever spark was lit at your job interview is now lost. The top 20 percent of your intellectual power, which could make the difference in innovation, is now directed into searching for your next job. Moreover, your team—and its potential power—just got smaller and weaker. You all still show up physically yet your "out of sight" power is turned off.

And, ultimately, the employee gives notice or is eventually asked to leave. The announcement goes out. The desk is empty. Everyone already knew that it was only a matter of time for the "body" to follow the heart and mind that had left months ago. And this departure is only the tip of the iceberg. Others will follow. And, the short- and even mid-term impact will force change at the top.

So what needs to happen?

Organizations can be the ones to create the changes needed to create an environment that fosters connection and engagement. Leaders can be proactive by getting to the root of the discomfort with vulnerability that is creating this stagnation instead of waiting to react to ad hoc pressure points when an employee gives notice. If the first sign of disengagement is closing one's heart to connection with colleagues, teams, and an organization's cause—then leaders can take preemptive action to create an environment that attracts, nurtures, and retains people through their heart. Yet this requires a new way of thinking and willingness to fight.

A great example of this was a client of ours who worked with an international oil distribution company. He was one of the three divisional presidents and called us about delivering a routine "team building" experience for his leadership team. In our discovery, the team was incredibly siloed. They worked remotely around the world. There was little connection between them and, even worse, a lack of interest or desire to connect. As one director put it, "It's a waste of time for me. I don't need any of them to be successful at what I do in my job. So what's the point?" As we dug deeper, we found that there was also a deep skepticism between the presidents; they believed that anything they wanted to do divisionally would have zero impact on the overall organization, because the CEO of the company was authoritarian with his decisions and generally not open to others' suggestions. So each of the divisional leaders had checked out of the larger organization and disconnected with their peers, pushing through with only their departments' responsibilities.

To fast forward, the one-time "team building" experience turned into quarterly divisional offsites and one-on-one executive coaching with the divisional president. All of these efforts turned his division into the company's top performer from the perspective of revenue and EBITDA (earnings before interest, taxes, depreciation, and amortization). This led to two other divisional presidents bringing us in for coaching and team development. Even the CEO began to become more open as we facilitated leadership offsites with him and with his three divisional presidents. The entire culture shifted to become more connected and open, which has continued to drive greater overall performance.

We Don't Know What We Don't Know

Embracing authenticity is a new paradigm for corporate culture. Authenticity, aligned with purpose, hasn't been a focus for organizations. Most leaders haven't known that this is the gateway to unleashing the true power of their organization.

Emotional intelligence (EQ) has certainly been embraced over the last decade. Your EQ is now considered to be as important as your IQ. However, having emotional intelligence does not guarantee that you are authentic. It's more than that. While the greater your emotional intelligence the more authentic you can be, authenticity in the workplace simply means "you being you"—but it is not always simple to bring to life. Can you show up with your ideas and opinions—with the emotional context included—and be respected and accepted for what you bring to the organization? Or do you govern yourself for fear of rejection?

Even if you have some way to understand and communicate what emotion is triggered by a situation, you're still not sure where we go from here. So what? How do you translate this skill into a bottom-line result? Even among the leaders that embrace emotional intelligence as a required skillset, most still don't know how to leverage EQ into true power for the organization by being authentic themselves and by promoting authenticity in their corporate culture.

The paradigm shift is from emotional intelligence to authenticity. Authenticity is the key to unleashing power.

In our preparation working with leaders and teams, we elicit input from each of them. Commonly, everyone (with the exception of the HR director) will make a comment such as "I hope this isn't some kind of touchy-feely-kumbaya process." Then, as we get into the work, we do an exercise, where we lay out 250 pictures of all kinds of things—work pictures, financial statement pictures, sports teams, family, beach, mountains, and more. We then ask team members to look at all the pictures and select the ones that resonate the most with them emotionally. Invariably, most come back with the pictures representing family or vacation areas, places that speak to non-work environments: pictures that carry a significant emotional component of love and joy, passion and peace. When the team members reflect on the nature of the pictures, there is a common "aha" moment—we are people on a team who love our spouses and families, enjoy hobbies and recreation, and in general we represent more than just work. They have just shared the other domains of their lives that are truly important, leading to comments like "Wow, I've worked with you for ten years and I didn't know those things about you!"

These teams just didn't know that there was more to the person's story that was relevant to the workplace. They didn't know that getting to know a person, where they've been and what kind of life they've had, makes a difference in understanding how they may show up and take positions on a business issue. They didn't know about the interests that they share with their teammates, be it favorite hobbies, age of children, or common vacation themes, which only deepens their sense of connection with each other. They didn't know that when they are able to express and even show emotion, positive or negative, it doesn't alienate their colleagues, but allows them to be drawn into a real connection with them, not because they are interested intellectually, but because they have connected with them from the heart.

Don't worry if you fear you have low emotional intelligence because you can still be authentic just by being transparent. If you grew up in a home where emotions were suppressed and now, as an adult, you are first learning to develop EQ—share it. Tell your coworkers that you value emotional intelligence because you believe it will help you connect with people. By sharing the story of your struggle, you are being authentic.

When you get to see someone for who she really is as a human being, beyond the façade, underneath the armor—not what they want you to know about them, but the true person—you can genuinely open yourself to their struggles on the job. You then develop empathy, compassion, and a feeling of care for your colleagues that comes from a genuine desire to support them with their challenges. That's because you're emotionally engaged with them and with their cause, not just intellectually curious. When someone is emotionally invested in a cause, it brings out their greatest sense of creativity, inspiration, and motivation to support solutions. You will do whatever you can, whatever is necessary, to bring real support.

That is authenticity in the workplace at its best. So what are we doing today that will deepen our level of connection?

A Little, Yet Not Enough: Need for Cultural Innovation

When we first started in our practice, we seldom heard the word "emotion," and certainly never in the context of intelligence. Thankfully, today most businesses and teams embrace emotional intelligence. As we visit new office designs, we find more open seating structures that support flatter (less hierarchical) organizations aspiring to work outside traditional boundaries through a matrix of collaboration. This is a little change in the right direction, but it is not enough.

Here's an example of why a little change is not enough, highlighted in the distinction between two types of teams that reach out to us for teamwork support.

In the first case, we're asked to facilitate a one-day offsite to help the team engage at a higher level by identifying the challenges with the team dynamic and developing a solution so the team can function on all cylinders. It's a one-day, one-time engagement that we receive in a transactional context: a beginning and an end in one day. We do the preparation work, facilitate the group to deepen its connections, finish up with exercises to help them anchor and integrate the experience— and then we all go home. We get positive reviews and the day seems like a rewarding experience for everyone who participated. But afterward, the teams will go back to their default rhythms, and when we check back a few months later, we find that little has changed. Though the offsite earned good grades for the day, there was no long-term impact. These results are not surprising.

The first team intellectually knew that investing in teamwork is an important part of the plan, and it was able to check off "teamwork" on the tactical checklist for the year. Yet, although helpful, the value of the one-day offsite we facilitated was limited. It's okay. Teamwork is not a tactical event; it's a strategic, ongoing process.

In the second scenario, we are engaged by the CEO to develop vision and strategy for co-creating a real team to carry out its mission. We launch with a three-day intense offsite to map out the biggest picture we can envision as well as the framework to bring it to life. We stir things up, lots of emotions—from fear to excitement; from frustration to hopefulness— and we come out on the other side with awareness that they have only just started coming together as a real team. We're invited to coach them in weekly phone sessions, and we visit their offices each quarter for two full days of individual, team, and breakout explorations and meetings. Each builds on the last and sets us up for the next progress point: we co-create a success record. It is an intentional process that speaks to an authentic relationship by and among us as coaches, the leader, and the team. We do not put a name on it right away, but we all are thinking the same thing—there is a newly discovered and recovered power coming from the connections that are driving and inspiring us as a team.

The second team knew instinctively that investing in teamwork is strategic, and the value we helped introduce continues to grow. If we're going to connect to the power, then we need to fight for it on an ongoing basis; it's not an isolated event, it's a process that changes the culture.

By working for INpowerment, we're calling for a cultural revolution. Revolutions are inspired because people have a cause worth fighting for. The cause here is to find, claim, and use the power that is already inside—inside each member of the team, and by extension inside the team. Power sitting idle. Power screaming for attention and attraction. Power to reach inside, grab, and embrace individual gifts and genius. Power to uplift members of their team. Power to connect to something bigger than the individual. Power from authentic connection.

Bigger Than Me

The key to aligning teams around a common purpose is to understand that people yearn to be a part of something bigger than themselves. They want to be part of something that matters, something significant and meaningful—because they want to feel like their life has meaning and significance. We all do!

When we are focused on ourselves, and create a "me-centered universe," then we feel like it's us against the world. We become paranoid and believe everyone is out to "get me." We create our own goals and objectives and feel a temporary sense of accomplishment as we check things off our to-do list or attain accolades and trappings of success. We may even feel that we've arrived! But in the end, the adrenaline wears off, as if it were a fix from our most recent accomplishment, leaving us desperately unfulfilled and on the treadmill for the next fix.

When we can connect to a greater purpose or something outside ourselves, we will be motivated on behalf of the "cause" and do whatever we can to move that cause forward. We involve ourselves with this cause because there is an alignment with our own personal sense of purpose and what's in our core beliefs.

As organizations struggle with their cultural revolution, connecting individuals to a purpose becomes one of the first steps in the process. This connection may come from the CEO and senior management if they identify the purpose of the organization in its mission statement.

But mission is not purpose. So, many times, we start with the senior leadership team to understand why the company exists. This reason is at the core of the purpose for the organization. Even though the annual report may read as though the purpose of the organization is to increase shareholder value, we see that as an outcome flowing from the purpose rather than the purpose itself.

For example, we once had clients who ran an automotive retail organization. When we first asked them what the purpose for their business was, they predictably said, "to sell cars." So, we explored what was underneath their culture and focus, how they approached customer service, and then we analyzed their interactions with employees and vendors. Below the surface of all these facets was a common belief that "every person is worthy!" When the leadership team gained this clarity and was able to articulate their purpose, they could begin to align personally and professionally around actions they could take to make that happen. These changes led the company on an eighteen-month record-breaking revenue and profitability streak, ending in the successful sale of the company. Their record-breaking car sales were the result of aligning with their purpose—not because they were focused on the bottom line.

Purpose can also show up as a departmental need. Each department needs to be clear about what their purpose is, to explore exactly what concept under the umbrella of the corporate purpose relates specifically to their function. Whether it's finance, marketing, sales, operations, or human resources, each has a departmental purpose that aligns everyone on its team. Purpose can also show up on committees or task forces, pulled together to investigate a particular challenge or opportunity. Purpose can come from community initiatives that speak about how the organization's purpose is meant to carry out its sense of community responsibility. It may be that the organization chooses to align itself with a particular charity. Again, creating a departmental extension of the organizational purpose to charity provides another connection for the team and you.

These are all points of connection and alignment to something greater than yourself that will invoke your deepest sense of desire and, just as important, fulfillment in the accomplishment. When you feel that you have done something meaningful, you know how different the sense of joy and fulfillment feels. When you clean out your closet, you can be happy to check that task off your list. When you take your clothes and donate them to a local charity and see the faces of the men and women who benefit, you feel a deep sense of gratitude for the opportunity to make a difference.

Every vocational role has the opportunity to be part of and connect to something that is greater than the role itself. And every role has the capacity to generate incremental power (or value) by being part of something greater—this is the magic of synergy. The source of that untapped power comes from an authentic connection to ourselves and other members of the team.

An individual is part of a larger team, yet sometimes he or she can feel they're operating in a silo, disengaged from contributing to and receiving value from colleagues. This aloneness perpetuates from and among the team members and is strengthened by a lack of authenticity and connection. All parties yearn for authentic connection—both to their own passion and the shared vision of the team.

Fulfillment will create loyalty and a long-term commitment to an organization, more than just working for a paycheck. Passionate and shared fulfillment makes you want to get up in the morning, get to work, and do something meaningful—to bring the best of yourself to work that day. You may not know how, but you sure want to do something with this inspiration and power that you feel inside.

It's Already INside

There is a funny thing about INspiration—it comes from INside us! There is something that moves us INternally, at our core—a sweet feeling that brings out joy and hope, at times tenderness, even tears of desire, that all lead to an extraordinary level of creativity, commitment, and motivation. There may be an external stimulant that has evoked our INspiration, but what's touching is definitely deeply withIN us.

So where do we get this power?

The destination is within and inside each of us. Yet the full power resides inside the team when its members show up with their power. The journey calls for us to return to the magical source of our authentic connection.

That is why we are so focused on individual and group INpowerment. For sure, empowerment is not a new concept. In fact, many times the term is overused as a cliché for teams. The problem with empowerment is that the notion of how to empower individuals and teams too often misses the critical element of authenticity. In fact, we believe that empowerment is unattainable, or at least unsustainable, without authenticity being its core component.

That is why we prefer the term INpowerment—we have to always look internally first before we can look externally. We have to be all IN, and willing to be the beautifully imperfect beings we are. We have to be willing to share our diverse set of perspectives, to use our own unique voice.

We have to be IN our personal power. Power comes from authenticity. Power comes from showing up. Power comes from dissenting with the status quo because you have a different take. Power comes from speaking to an elephant that you believe is in the room. Power comes from asking for help. Power comes from helping others that you see need extra support. Power comes from you, getting outside of a "me" perspective and getting aligned with something greater than yourself.

All of these elements of power are what we believe is true INpowerment.

Empowerment many times connotes waiting for others to support you to be all that you can be. INpowerment requires a shift to claim personal responsibility to do what you need to find alignment with something greater than yourself, show up with your voice, and bring your personal power to the team.

The only obstacle to accessing that power is our judgment about what we cannot be or do.

Once we let go of our self-limiting beliefs, we let IN Power.

When teams ask us to help them reenergize because they're stale or going through the motions, we'll bring them together for a day and challenge them through a series of exercises to "let go" of the weight they've been unknowingly carrying. This weight consists of challenges, concerns, conflicts, and fears—all of which create a heavy belief system that thwarts access to their potential. As individuals and then as a team, they release their burdens by sharing their concerns, and the energy transforms from heavy to light, from limited to unlimited, from stale to powerful.

They realize that the power was there the whole time. They just didn't know where to look. By taking stock of the heaviness of self-limiting beliefs, they were able to unload the myths about what was holding them back and return to what was always theirs to claim—the power to connect to their truth, passion, sovereign wants, and to the vision they hold for themselves and their realm. They were able to connect to their core truths while being free and unencumbered from self-doubt, self-deception, and unspoken blessings. They are INpower.

We yearn for a return to our instinctive and natural soulful connections—to our own passion and the authentic being of others. Because this is where unlimited power resides. This is where the hope for those people comes to life. They have a sense—either consciously or unconsciously—that they and their colleagues are leaving capacity, energy, or power on the table. They want to claim the energy and change that will come from shifting their relationship to and with themselves and the team.

The opportunity is to look inside—beyond the self-talk that keeps us from our enormous power. INpower and ready to listen to the voice that will change the old recording—I can't, I shouldn't, or I won't—to the new message: I can and I will.

The destination is very close, indeed—but it still takes a journey to get there. Start now.

CHAPTER 3

Break Through: Claim Responsibility to Shift Direction

· · · · · ·

The Choice

DO YOU WANT to change because where you are is painful? Do you want to move forward, but can't seem to find a way out of your current situation? There is no way "out"—but there is a way "IN."

Teams and individuals who feel disconnected from true potential and purpose—feeling frustrated with themselves and with their connection to the team—begin to recognize that they need to make a different choice to expect a different outcome. The classic definition of insanity is to do the same thing over and over and expect a different result. It's time to choose to do something different! This choice is yours to make.

Many people want to make this change. Many of the leaders and teams that we work with say that they stay up at night worried about what is blocking them, trying to develop a clear plan to break through the chaos or move forward instead of going through the motions. They are tired of the constant in-team backstabbing and desperately want to shift to having each other's backs.

They are the people who are prepared to take responsibility for their role in their current situation and are ready to confront challenges so they can shift from blaming others on their team to helping their team become stronger. The pain of the status quo has become greater than the pain associated with change, and this has created a catalyst to do something different.

What blocks us from making these choices are our self-limiting beliefs, starting with the ones about whether we have any choice or ability to create change. Frankly, when you feel like you're stuck, you may feel like you have no choice. You feel like you are a victim and believe this is your lot, your place in life. The truth is that you *do* have a choice. There may be consequences to your choices, but you have a choice nonetheless.

You could leave. Leaving is always an option. But what you're likely to find is that you are back in the same situation—this time at a different company. This is because you only changed your external surroundings, not the internal problem, the root of the issue—which means in some ways you've gone deaf, mute, and dead. You have lost YOU! You have let go of what's important to yourself. You stopped trying to beat your head against the wall and caved in to the force of the almighty status quo.

You need to reclaim your ME! You need to choose to fully step back into your life. You need to find your voice again. You need to ignite your internal passions and inspiration. This is your choice. Your option. Your life!

Find Your Lost Voice

So, if you have choice, what are your options?

You can maintain the status quo, go through the motions, and wait for something better to happen—hoping that an outside force will change your situation. Or, you can look for your power to change the situation. Where is your power? You haven't seen it in a while. Maybe you forgot you ever had it, or . . .

Have you given your power away? To whom have you given it?

To your boss. To your board. To your family. To your staff. Perhaps you have given your power away to all of them. Always looking for a way to serve and support others and your business, you have forgotten about taking care of yourself. And, by rendering yourself last in place, you're actually less effective as a helper. It has become a way of life.

Why did this happen to you? Or, why did you let this happen to you? Fear drives your voice underground. You let others override your voice because you are afraid of being rejected. Slowly and surely, you stop speaking out, fail to set personal boundaries, and effectively give implicit permission for others to substitute your voice with theirs. You do this to yourself because you want to be accepted and fear that you will be excluded from the conversation if you stand out or speak up.

The paradox is that you are actually keeping yourself from the conversation. You have already given your power away.

A leader came to us asking for help in reconciling why he was passed over for promotion. We learned that his firm had gone through a series of mergers attendant with layoffs, and though he survived, he was afraid there was a risk that he might be let go. As a result, he stayed under the radar screen; he kept his head down and his voice low. He was passed over. What he needed to do was put his head up, raise his voice, be seen and heard—despite the risk. Once he made this shift, his relationship with the CEO dramatically changed and he received the next promotion. He found his power.

Without your power, you are stuck. Stuck with this nagging feeling you sense in your body. Although the feeling is always present, you are so familiar with it that you've even stopped noticing it exists. You've silenced your own voice.

The nagging feeling is your lost voice trying to scream out, "I have lost touch with what's important to me!" You are out of alignment with your belief system, with your values, with what you want most in your life. You hate it!

By screaming it out, you remove layers of built-up sludge that has suppressed your voice—the gateway to your power. By clearing out that persistent block, you create space for your true power to emerge. The only way you can get back to your integrity and authentically connect with your belief system, values, and sovereign needs, is to reclaim your lost voice.

You need to let yourself reconnect to what's lost inside, to cry for what is missing, what you long for. Whether offering the feedback in a meeting that you held back in the past or offering a bold and unconventional idea, you need to shift from accepting that your lost voice is a way of life to admitting to yourself that you have a voice—and then declaring that you want it back. This is the breakthrough to unleash your power.

Change Starts from WithIN

Now that you've realized you want your voice back, the journey can begin. This is a journey back to YOU. Classically, we look outside ourselves for answers and change, hoping to find a cure for the aching pit in our stomachs. But searching outside hasn't led you to a sense of passion and fulfillment in your life. It's only left you less than whole—a partial you.

You must go inside and embrace that the change you must make begins with you. It's not the team that has to change. It's not your boss. It's not your commute. It's not your kids. It's *you*.

Exploring why and how you lost your true connection is at the core of your journey. When you have lost your connection to yourself, you have lost touch with the many things that make you who you are— your values and beliefs, your wants and desires, and what you are most passionate about. You have sacrificed your joy to the incessant drone of the status quo.

This lack of connection to self is the chief culprit responsible for your loss of power. How can you expect to be at your best, to bring your inspiration and creativity, to share the synergies that you find in meaningful debate and conversation, if you are disconnected from yourself? You can't! We can't. Nobody can! There is a voice deep inside that knows you can offer more value and ideas; yet you are not doing these things. This can be a source of deep shame, resentment, and frustration, because you are out of touch first and foremost with yourself.

Let's face it. Most of us are far more critical of ourselves than we are of others. So there is a part of you deep down that is just beating yourself up and is your own worst critic. These constant criticisms can take your wind out of your sails. You may lack the fight to do something about your situation, so you get smaller and smaller, giving away more and more of your power.

That is because until now, you haven't known WHAT to do to change your situation or HOW to do it. That's why you are reading this book! We are showing you the pathway through—this path is INward.

As you begin to take this step inward, you will begin to see choices about how you can get back into integrity with yourself first, and then with the team. As you reclaim your own connection to yourself, and show up more in your power, you are automatically getting back into integrity—into wholeness—with the team.

Said another way, being aligned with the team starts by being aligned with yourself.

Claiming Responsibility

The change you want to see starts with you claiming responsibility for making it happen.

When we interview team members before an offsite, we hear a myriad of excuses: "If only we could get rid of Bob, we'd be okay," or "The problem is the boss; if only she did the right thing we'd be fine," or "If only the home office understood the challenges we face in the field." Casting blame on others is the default for team members when they misdiagnose problems in the hopes of finding easy solutions. Although there may be some truth in this feedback process, it will not help to change any situation. It may even exacerbate the problem as team members become defensive when they sense they are being attacked or blamed.

There is an alternative approach.

Instead of waiting for someone else to take the lead, you need to claim responsibility for your part in creating a bad situation . . . and your part in getting out of it. You need to ask, "How did I get us here? What did I do to contribute to the situation? Things just don't happen to me; I must have had a part in creating it."

Once you open yourself to the possibility that you are responsible for creating the "stuckness," you have the opportunity to change. You got yourself here; now you need to get yourself out.

By claiming responsibility for your part in creating the challenge and doing your part to work through it, you serve as a role model. When all of your team follows this formula, you will co-create success. The impact of your behavior will inspire others to claim responsibility for their roles. They will shift from blaming others and you to claiming their roles in becoming stronger with the team—so as a group they no longer point fingers at each other. They can use that valuable energy toward a positive purpose. They start to encourage and support each other to own their parts and roles in co-creating a successful outcome. The pain of the status quo has become greater than the pain associated with change, and therefore is a catalyst to do something different.

This concept is not a difficult one to understand, though each time we work with teams the lightbulb of new awareness goes off. Intellectually, it's easy to understand; yet it's difficult to implement.

Teams are concerned about how to bring it back home and often ask us for help in doing this.

Let's Go. I'm Ready!

When you embrace the fact that you hold the key to making changes, you stop being a victim and take back your power to change your world. All you need to do is choose to connect and engage with all of your truth.

Now it is up to you.

To hold this power is both exciting and scary. It's exciting to see a path to reclaiming who you are and all that you have to offer, now that you know you hold the key to this change. The hope that you feel on this path will bring you a greater sense of passion, inspiration, and fulfillment.

The flip side of this excitement is anxiety. Change is always challenging, especially when you take full responsibility for yourself and the changes that you want to make. This journey will take you into some unchartered territory, so it's appropriate to have some anxiety about the process.

You need to embrace both ends of the emotional spectrum as you choose to connect and engage with yourself and your team.

Once you make the decision, you need to take action. The fear will tug at your sleeves, and attempt to pull you back into a spiral of second-guessing. Acknowledge it, be thankful that the presence of the emotion keeps you grounded, and then move through it. The more you become comfortable with the gray area of the emotional swing, the more power you access each time you choose to move forward.

Overcoming the challenge of change is one of the ways that we grow most. Think about it. Do you grow more when all is going smoothly, or when you are going through some type of adversity? As necessity is the mother of invention, so is it necessary for you to reinvent yourself. The difference is that you don't have to reinvent yourself by trying to be someone that you aren't—you just need to reclaim yourself and be all of who you already are.

The best part of this new awareness is that you are completely in charge. You do not have to wait on anybody else. You don't have to get anybody's approval. There is nothing and no one to slow you down. You can start today, right now, and begin making different choices in your life.

So why wait?

Start now. Choose to begin the process of learning more about you. Choose to engage with yourself and others more fully and completely. Start looking inside to find your voice and learn where you can connect with something greater than yourself. Start looking inside for your passion. Start taking responsibility for your choices, attitudes, and levels of engagement.

Start right now!

When you begin to take responsibility for yourself differently, you will begin to see shifts in how your team engages and responds to you. They may be puzzled at first, not knowing this "new" you. But now they don't have to relate to the "victim you" who had been doing nothing more than going through the motions at work. As they connect with the "new you," it will actually begin to stir them up, as they secretly desire to have what you have. They will see you "comfortable in your own skin," more INpowered, speaking up in discussions and taking risks to share your perspective.

This inspiration sparks the beautiful process of allowing everyone to begin to make new choices for themselves. Everyone on the team may begin to see a different way to connect and interact. These changes create a stronger sense of alignment with everyone as they connect to a meaningful and shared goal.

To get these results, all you did was change the only thing that you have any control over—YOU!

So, let's go! Are you ready?

CHAPTER 4

All Are Invited:
The Time Is NOW!

· · · · · · ·

The Team and the Individual

WHEN AN INDIVIDUAL shows up INpowered, a new vision for the team can emerge. Once the team recognizes the positive impact these INpowered and energetic individuals have, the team is stirred up, excited about new opportunities, and curious about what needs to happen for the whole team to become INpowered.

It can be new, even revolutionary, to see someone who is open and transparent, someone who speaks with confidence and power. It can be confusing, challenging, and even scary. The team may ask a lot of questions as they move forward: "How can each of us take on this new energy? How can we be like this all of the time? How can we as individuals take responsibility to show up differently and then come together as a team in service to each other? What is the difference between my role as an individual and my part as a member of the team?"

Everyone must examine themselves, the team, and their relationship to the team in an entirely new way. Once each team member reaches inside himself or herself and shares their real truth in real time with each other, an INpowered team can start to come alive.

Yet the reality that there can be dysfunction in the individual and in the culture of the team may stand in the way of openness. This transparency may still be rejected, even when it is proven to be effective or its power is displayed. Even though it seems all team members are on board academically and viscerally, they may still be having an internal battle going on. In order for the team to embrace the revolution, we need to explore what lies underneath and drives these common dilemmas and dysfunctions.

Common Dilemmas

Here are some familiar scenarios within organizations that contribute to disconnection and a lack of performance:

Talent Isn't Enough

A CEO client of ours assembled his team with the best class of individual talent, but this team failed to connect and engage—and as a result ultimately became dysfunctional.

The CEO successfully recruited top talent to all the key positions. Each individual recognized the impressive talent of their colleagues. Yet the CEO and the team had a sense that something wasn't right with performance in regard to all the team members' potential—and none of them could identify the source of the dysfunction.

When we worked with them to analyze this problem, we discovered there was no eye contact at their meetings, and it was clear that self-survival governed team results. The elephants in the room were becoming terrifyingly familiar, although no one dared speak up about the underlying tension.

The team discussions focused on constraints that came from each other's self-limiting beliefs. Instead of getting energy from each other when the team got together, they actually drained power from one another. Everyone was losing sleep. The CEO was ready to give up on himself unless he could figure out how to leverage the untapped power of the team.

The limiting assumption of the CEO and team members was that functional talent was all it took to succeed. Instead each member needed to invite the power inside themselves to connect with the other team members' power. The talent that the CEO recruited was hiding in independent silos, and the opportunity to leverage the team's collective power was lost. Only by openly engaging the talent in an authentic and collaborative operating model would the world-class recruits become a world-class team.

Compete or Collaborate

We worked with a law firm that struggled as its partners competed with each other rather than share and leverage their wealth and wisdom.

The firm's individual partners kept their respective clients confidential, refusing to share the identity of their clients out of fear that if they shared access, their partners might steal away the client relationship. By clinging tenaciously to these client relationships, these partners missed the opportunity to cross-fertilize and leverage their relative strengths in order to maximize the best interests of the clients and the firm.

The shift needed was for the partners to overcome the self-limiting belief that other partners would steal their clients, and instead embrace the opportunity that when each partner shares, the firm grows and all its partners become stronger.

Outside the Boardroom

The challenge to connect with our inner strength and to others is found everywhere, even in religious institutions and among volunteers on non-profit boards.

Working with volunteer boards—whether for causes or religious institutions—we have experienced individual fractured agendas and interests among the members become the focus rather than the shared vision of the entire organization.

Only when the volunteers authentically connect with the other volunteers, and together align to the cause and vision of the organization they all serve will the board be filling its purpose.

There Is a Way Out!

Now that you've connected with the contrast of the old—closed, indifferent, and disconnected—versus the new way of operating—open, caring, and connected—you are either eager to figure out how to get there or skeptical that it's possible. Perhaps even a little of both.

The important message is that you need to embrace the journey. Journeys are rarely straight lines. They meander like a stream, turning left and right, even doubling back to reverse course for some period, before returning to their ultimate destination. But you need to keep answering the challenge of INpowerment every day and stay committed to this new way of thinking if you want to see results.

There are milestones along the way that will help you take stock of how far you've come. You will notice that a thorny conflict with a colleague that had not been confronted in the past is now being addressed and resolved with understanding. You'll observe your team supporting a teammate who has a personal situation that restricts him from dealing with a project; previously, the teammate would have kept the personal issue private and the team would have silently sat in judgment about his behavior.

Because this is a journey that will take you into unchartered territory, there will also be hazards that remind you of the difficulty in changing. Just know they are milestones that affirm you are doing this right. Although you may occasionally fall back into the old and comfortable way of interacting with others, you will also catch yourself and notice the difference between retreating into your silo and becoming INpowered. When you acknowledge the distinction, you also remember that the new way is a better choice, though these new behaviors will probably not stick overnight.

It will be scary, and maybe even dangerous, as you break new ground in the process of reclaiming all that you are. You may fear being rejected. It is painful to not be accepted. The danger is that you are allowing people to truly know you, your beliefs, ideas, perspectives; and rather than embracing you, they may choose to distance themselves from you—or worse, use this intimate information against you.

The self-limiting beliefs are likely front and center for you. The words "I can't" may be all too present. You may think, "I can't collaborate because it's a waste of time. I can't share my clients because the other partners will take them from me. I can't cross the aisle because my party will see me as weak. I can't step into the hard conversation with my spouse because, well, it's too hard. I can't because these people don't have the same vision as I do."

Staying on the path requires a leap of faith. Whenever we are uncertain about a direction, we can't mitigate all of the risks or even know what all the risks are until we get underway. We have to have faith that those that have preceded us were the trailblazers, and if it worked for them, it can work for us, too. Know that you have tried other ways to find deeper fulfillment before, and yet, here you are—a limited version of all that you could be.

So, even though there may be risks, there is a place deep inside you that says, "No matter what, I have to do this!"

Sir Ernest Henry Shackleton was an Anglo-Irish explorer in the early 1900s. He led three expeditions to the Antarctic in search of the South Pole. According to *Discerning History*, he ran the following ad in the local paper, looking for men to join him on his quest:

> MEN WANTED: For hazardous journey, small wages, bitter cold, long months of complete darkness, constant danger, safe return doubtful, honor and recognition in case of success.

Shackleton received an overwhelming amount of responses to this advertisement!

While the quest we're promoting in this book is for men and women, it does require you to connect with the adventurous part of yourself, which will help you find your bravery and courage.

Trust that the process will get you there. Trust that the growth and lessons along the way will bring you enormous amounts of fulfillment and gratitude. Trust that the stream ultimately has a destination, and that destination is for you to be completely connected to all that you are and completely, authentically engaged with yourself and your team.

This is the way out of your self-imposed prison and the way forward to an engaged and fulfilling life!

CHAPTER 5

Who Goes First: Don't Look Outside Yourself for the Leader

· · · · · ·

Who Goes First?

THE JOURNEY TO INpowerment is for individuals and their teams. Ultimately, transformed individuals build powerful teams, and a powerful team inspires individuals. The two serve each other. An INpowered team helps the next new member to become INpowered, and an INpowered individual can bring change to the team. Like the chicken-and-egg conundrum, it doesn't matter which comes first, though both must take the journey together through this book.

Most people assume that embracing a deeper level of authenticity, especially when you are changing the culture of an organization, must start with the head of the organization or team. However, our experience shows that though hierarchal leaders need to buy into the benefits and be willing to become authentic in order for the shift in the organization to be sustainable, the catalyst for that change can actually come from anyone on the team.

We've seen a spark come from the most junior member of the team, a newbie who had not yet been indoctrinated into the existing culture of the organization. At an annual managers' offsite that we facilitated, several of the seasoned members came with a "wait and see what the boss does" attitude, clearly a learned survival skill from their prior experience interacting at group meetings; meanwhile, the newest member had the courage to speak what was on her mind.

During one of our exercises designed to help create awareness of elephants in the room (unspoken tensions), she stepped up first and spoke about a critical problem that she saw: how managers communicate. She described how she felt about the impact this problem had on her and her performance, and she asked for what she wanted from the team. Her act of leadership opened a three-hour session of candid sharing that shaped the dynamic of the offsite. When we designed this exercise before the meeting, we knew that we were setting the team up for a breakthrough; we just didn't know how—or from whom—it would begin.

Everyone on the team is a leader, and anyone—not just the hierarchal boss—can step into his power and begin the process of change.

Boss v. Leader

It's important that we distinguish the difference between a boss and a leader. The boss is the person who owns the ultimate decision. They are accountable for a particular decision. In a management team, the boss may be the functional expert that has authority over a specific domain. The CFO is the boss over accounting issues. The HR Director is responsible for employee-related issues. The COO will have final say on product delivery. The President or CEO will have the final decision about key areas of strategy and other management issues that have reached a stalemate between department heads.

A leader can be anyone on the team—anyone, including the boss. That's because everyone has something to offer. Leaders bring their power to the team—their voice that shares their ideas, opinions, and concerns. Everyone who exercises his or her personal power in this way is a leader.

Most of us have been caught in the cultural context of hierarchical organizational models. Some of us may have been exposed to an organizational model based on more of a matrix. Both of these have implied leadership roles, based on position. Obviously different responsibilities come with different positions. But a work team is like a football team: each position has its roles and responsibilities.

You may be under the impression that if you don't have people reporting to you, then you are NOT a leader. That's just not true! Even if your role does not require you to have people reporting to you, you are still a leader. You are in your organization for a reason. You are giving your life energy and skills to your company. You are meant to bring all that you have to the team, and operate at the peak of your abilities. In this way, you are absolutely a leader!

While the boss may have the final decision, you owe it to yourself—and your team—to bring all that you have to discussions and meetings. There are many times where management team members wait for the boss to take the lead or defer to his/her direction without completely expressing their views. That shift can begin with any leader on a team, not just the hierarchal boss. Anyone who is in his or her power can play a leadership role. When you are in your power and truly own it, you step into your individual leadership and speak your truth, disrupt the toxic rhythm, and inspire others to follow outside their comfort zone.

Neither the organization nor the boss can grant you the power of the leadership that is already inside you. You must give yourself permission to exercise your power as a leader. Anytime you withhold your ideas, opinions, or viewpoints, you're not only cheating yourself, but you're cheating your team. The most effective bosses know that the best team is one filled with leaders.

Yet, there are bosses who don't actually want to have "leaders" on their teams. Rather, they like to be the director of all activities and look for people to do what they are told. In these environments, you will ultimately have to choose between staying in your role (with practical limitations to your power) or changing environments (which may not always be a practical option).

There are also times when the boss intentionally builds an environment of authenticity by leaving his "controlling authority" behind by being an "open leader." An example of this kind of approach was taken by a CEO who kicked off one of our management offsites by saying, "Hey guys, I really want us to completely show up with whatever each person has to bring. I want you to challenge me, and others, if you have a different opinion. I want you to express with complete candor any issues that are limiting your ability to be successful, especially if I'm the one impacting you!"

Here, the CEO is inviting everyone to bring their power, their voice. He is doing so not by being just the boss, but by being a leader, too.

Everyone Can Be a Leader

When you are INpowered, you are a leader. Through the leadership of INpowerment, you will influence and guide others, even if they do not report to you and bring the vision of the team to fruition. You'll also inspire others to follow your model.

Everyone has the capacity to be a leader; and the authority for this power is inside everyone.

Once you buy into the premise that each of us can be a leader, the next step is to give yourself permission to tap into that power. Not so easy. First, you need to overcome the self-limiting belief that you do not have the authority to access it. Put another way, you do not have to wait for the boss to give you direction or grant you permission. Instead, believe you are the boss of you, and only you can control when you access your power to lead.

If you continue to resist this notion as foreign and unobtainable, let's further define what we mean by a leader.

A leader inspires others by serving as a role model, sometimes going first and other times listening from behind. A leader innovates either through fresh ideas or by courageously starting the process of opening up by showing vulnerability. The fountainhead of leadership is internal and its impact is external. A leader does not have to manage a team, or run a company, or be the boss. A leader emerges from the group because of their influence on others in the way they shape the team by expressing the power of their truth and insight.

Anyone can be the first one to offer an idea, or raise a counter or contrary view. Anyone can question the boss. Anyone can be the person who reads the energy in the room and then brings clarity to the team that it is going down the wrong track. Anyone can volunteer to show how she can be comfortable being uncomfortable and act as a role model for others. So, if anyone can do it, everyone can do it—even at the same time.

Once you start to imagine yourself as a leader—despite the position you play in the formal structure—you create limitless opportunity to bring your power to the life of the team you serve.

Leadership has many faces. It's as diverse as the members of a team. Ultimately, a team is at its best when everyone becomes a leader.

Stepping into Your Power Elevates Your Group's Power

When you take the risk to show up with all that you have, you are breaking the ice for others to do the same. In an unspoken way, you're giving everyone else permission to bring everything that they have to the situation. When that happens, your stepping in was the catalyst to bring the entire group to a new level.

Why is that?

The first person to find the courage to step in with all that they have to bring takes a risk. The risk is that they may be rejected by others on their team. When you're willing to get out of your comfort zone and take the risk to dive in with your truth, then everyone is pushed out of their comfort zones by having now to respond more openly and transparently.

This is what we call chaos. Chaos is simply when we have left a comfortable place for an uncomfortable place. There may be tension in the room. There may be a hard truth that was spoken. It may be that the elephant that has been taking up space in the middle of the room has now been named. It may be that conflict between members of the team is being expressed and openly dealt with. These situations are uncomfortable.

Chaos is typically what people try to avoid. We like things to feel nice and comfortable. But chaos is the gateway to getting the group to take another step toward unleashing the team's full power. So our mantra is "Embrace the Chaos!"

Chaos is critically important to every person and group. It's a fundamental step on the path to authenticity. Chaos is a crucial component to building trust. Think about it. If you never go through the fire together, then you never really get to build the trust that comes from knowing that you can come through together, and become stronger because of the challenge. Trust is built in part through shared experience. This is a very important shared experience the group needs to have.

In order to embrace the chaos, you have to find a way to trust the process, and to understand that each of your team members is here for the shared purpose of growing and becoming better leaders. If we can all embrace the chaos, then we will go into a place of discovery. This is a beautiful place of growth and learning for the individuals and for the group. You can learn how you react to tension, how you can find your voice in a discussion, how the group handles chaos, and information about each person on the team, including their motivations and desires.

On the other side of the chaos is a more deeply connected, tight, trusting, and authentic community of leaders. That's our goal. And it all started because you took a chance to show up differently. To show up fully and authentically—to show up in your power!

That leads us to an important leadership tenet:

Vulnerability is the gateway to
unleashing all of your power!

This idea may be completely counterintuitive. But vulnerability is leadership within a team. When you are in a place where it feels safe to become more vulnerable, and you show up with your truth, you are bringing your power to the team. That gives others on the team permission to do the same thing. Everyone in this leadership system is being vulnerable with who you are, your thoughts and opinions, ideas and wants, issues and concerns, opportunities and strategies. Everyone is open and authentically themselves.

This is different from the old-school belief about leadership that says leaders are people who have all the answers, are bulletproof, and have no feelings. In this belief, leaders are robots—in perfect control all the time.

Although there may still be times that it's important to be "big" with a broader audience and lead by inspiring and motivating others, when you are with your team, you can just be you. Sometimes you will be in a place of confidence and on a roll, and other times you will be anxious, scared, frustrated, overwhelmed, confused, or sad. That is what the team is there for: to help pick you up when you need it, and for you to pick up others when they are challenged.

Our client Eloise climbed the corporate ladder of success to become a Divisional COO of a paper manufacturing company by believing that she had to be the smartest person in the room with all of the answers for her team. However, in her new role, she often did not have the perfect solution to challenges. When we worked with her, she was struggling with how to reconcile tension between her sales and marketing chiefs. Once she failed in her attempts to resolve the conflict, she chose to ignore the growing problem that was now undermining the power of the team rather than to ask for support.

She gave us permission to facilitate a team meeting. We opened with a question for everyone to answer: "Share with the team a time when you were stuck and didn't know what to do. How did you ultimately overcome the block?"

We set it up for Eloise to go last. We watched her observe her team as they openly shared how each of them struggled when they were paralyzed with anxiety or frustration, and how difficult it was for them to admit they didn't know what to do, to accept they needed help, and to reluctantly seek it out. That depth of sharing paved the way for Eloise to show the courage of her vulnerability. She shared how she was taught as a young girl to be the best, the smartest, and to fix things without having to ask for help. Her revelation broke the barrier for her team to open up and offer their support. Both the sales and marketing chiefs were eager to help, and they ultimately worked out their differences as a result of Eloise showing that she was human.

So leadership within a team environment is actually being vulnerable and able to ask for help, support, and to share and challenge others in open, healthy debate. When you are willing to take the risk and make yourself vulnerable, the team will draw upon your example and the entire team, through its vulnerability, will unleash the power that comes from authenticity.

Dorothy's Slippers

Stepping into the power of leadership requires risk taking, truth telling, and becoming uncomfortable.

You have to be present first and foremost. You have to know where you are. You have to be aware of what you're feeling and be able to articulate that emotional context. You need to be clear about what you want and need from the team and its members in order to be most effective in what you're trying to accomplish.

If you want to thrive and unleash your power, you have to be "all in" to engage.

If you're going down the "yellow brick road" looking for your power, you can search forever. Instead, you must journey inside, deep down, to find the source of true power that is inside you and inside each one of us. You will find the infinite power to be, to lead, to inspire others—just by being the authentic you.

You are already wearing the magic slippers. You've always had them. You just need to be aware that you've stepped into them. Then take the first step. Take the step that brings your power to life—to your life and to the life of the team.

The power you want is inside yourself. This is to be INpowered.

We have worked with scores of leaders who got lost on the yellow brick road. One of our corporate clients asked us to work with an executive who was falling short of the CEO's expectations. He was timid about offering his opinions; instead he typically followed directions with a polite nod. He stammered from nerves when he made a presentation and appeared awkward in social situations with their customers. Yet the CEO had a hunch that the exec had much more power than he was bringing to the team. And after we met him, we agreed. Our work with him focused on inviting the client to see his power for himself, the power that his boss saw in him, and the reason he was hired.

He thought his slippers (responsibilities) were enormous and that his feet (abilities) were too small. We—and his boss—saw that he was the perfect fit for his shoes. But he had to wiggle and waggle, up and down, trying all sorts of new things, in someone else's backyard, fighting himself along the way, wrestling his biggest foe, the dark side within—especially fear—until he was able to get comfortable being uncomfortable inside what he perceived to be excessively large shoes (demands). This meant speaking up and out, even if first, and being contrary when he had a conviction about a position. Ultimately, he comfortably eased into his slippers with a knowing spirit that he had finally found inside himself. He found his power.

The great news is you are in complete control! You don't have to wait for anybody's permission to begin. You don't have to look outside your organization for the opportunity. You don't have to wait for your team-mates to agree to make a change.

This isn't about them. This is about you. This is about going deep inside and finding out who you really are and what you really want! What is important to you? What do you want to create for yourself? What do you want for and from the team?

You need to be willing to take a risk. That will take courage, but that's the next step. If you don't take the risk and you continue to with-hold who you are and the power of your contribution, then you will continue to die a thousand deaths from a lack of authentic connection and true fulfillment.

When you take the risk to step in and show up with all of who you are, with all of your unique gifts of thought, perspective, intellect, and experience, you embrace the fullness of who you are. This is a gift for any team. This is the power that ignites the team.

We all have it. Inside. This power is your very own pair of ruby red slippers—built for you. This is the power that you've had all along—you just didn't know it!

CHAPTER 6

Reclaim Your Power: Any and All Leaders IN

· · · · · ·

The Power Is Inside

MUCH OF THE time, people are looking for outside solutions, even though we know that we ourselves hold the key to resolving our issues. When high-potential teams are low performers, the solution may reside inside the team. Teams judge themselves based on external measures of performance that can create false pictures, rather than looking inside themselves for clarity of direction and value.

Classically, management philosophy has focused on two parallel tracks: how to grow revenues while controlling costs. The first is externally focused on marketing and sales initiatives. How do we grow market share within existing markets? How can we increase the close rate? How do we expand into new markets? How do we increase the pipeline of new opportunities? This is vitally important for every company.

Secondly, every company needs to have a clear handle on costs and to make prudent decisions about strategic investments and tactical expenditures. This needs to be a focus for everyone in the company, not just the senior executives.

In fact, most of the critical data on "dashboards" for management teams to review on a weekly basis incorporates these two areas of focus. The team looks at their pipeline, forecast of closed deals, sales, cost of goods sold, and other key sales or cost issues.

But to look *only* at these two areas is to miss the most important and possibly the ultimate key to sustainable success—how teams function internally. Are they operating openly, transparently, and with each person INpowered to show up and bring his or her true, authentic self? This is how the true power of an organization is unleashed.

External measurements can paint a false picture of how a team is performing. During the Great Recession of 2009, we worked with many CEOs who commented on how the boom times had masked their team's underlying issues. So even though you might close a huge deal, it doesn't mean that your management team is firing on all cylinders. Instead, you may have good sales people that are successful in spite of the organization's dysfunction.

Most of the management teams that we work with have very talented people. They just don't operate as a true, authentic team. They operate as a group of functional heads that know how to be successful inside of their own silo of control.

We want them to be successful with their functional teams, but no matter how successful they are, they can be even more so by focusing internally at breaking through the barriers between departments, both personally and as a team, to become an authentic community, aligned by the organization's purpose.

Missing the REAL Issue

Because leaders are often focused on these external results, teams often attempt to address symptoms rather than solving core issues.

Critics who attempt to understand why those teams fail often point to poor leadership and suggest the problem is a bad boss, lack of strategy, or the speed of execution. In reality, it's not necessarily true that the leaders are bad; it's that the leaders give up on themselves as they struggle for answers from outside forces they cannot control or influence.

It's a story they tell themselves based on their limiting belief that they can't find their way out of the problem. It becomes a self-fulfilling prophecy. Finally, after pointing fingers at every reason and person except themselves, they surrender to the idea that they cannot figure it out.

They complain that sales are down because of the economy. Production is slow and the cause is a strike in the supply chain. Turnover is up, so it's time to change the head of HR. Or perhaps the fault lies within the corporate strategy, so let's change that.

They're missing the core or real issues. They're looking externally for the power to change when all along the power is inside themselves and inside the very team sitting around the table.

A CEO engaged us to help their team address anemic sales. As we interviewed the team members, each one pointed to their challenges, including new competition, lack of product differentiation, ineffective ad campaigns, and issues with supply chain logistics.

Their choice had been to change strategy when things don't work. "We're going in the wrong direction," said the CEO.

We posited, "Well, maybe you're going in the correct direction, it's just that you're not moving—you're stuck. Perhaps it's the way your team has not come together in power and alignment. Rather than change strategy, let's look inward at the way you cohere as a group."

The solution is not about products, pricing, promotion—it's in the people who make the decisions, explore the options, co-create, innovate, and differentiate. The solution is about people and the way they engage as a team. You need to find the power within and cohere with the same belief that you will win.

It's easier to look externally and blame something outside of your control. You can wait for change, or you can look inside for what you can influence today.

The path to resolving the real issue is by reclaiming your power to lead.

Ultimately, the individuals found their power and became a team. They had been so convinced they were victims of circumstances they could not control that they forgot to look for and claim their internal power to influence how they responded. With reclaimed power, they repackaged their suite of services with compelling pricing and guarantees that got them back in the market; as a result, they blew away their competition.

Here's another story of how the leader of a team shifted the focus from looking externally for solutions to looking internally for inspiration.

We were referred to the owner/president of a struggling firm by his brother-in-law with whom we'd previously worked. The firm had been struggling with poor sales performance. To fix this issue, they banged their heads against the wall and tried new ad campaigns every three months, went through four sales managers in eighteen months, and nearly accepted a lowball offer to sell the business.

During an intense day with the owner, it became clear he was leading from a place of self-limiting beliefs. His story became the story by which everyone else on the team started—and it went downhill from there. Down the hill to all of the reasons why business was down, sales were slow, competition was fierce, regulation was tighter, banks were tougher, and talent harder to find and keep. Because the solutions of changing team members, ad agencies, banking arrangements, suppliers, and even law firms were clearly not working, the owner was ready to give up on himself.

This was the key to finding the solution. Because, for the first time, he was turning to the REAL source of the problem: himself. The same place that he was going to blame for the circumstances was actually the source of power to get out of the jam.

He had thought that he needed to have all of the answers all of the time, the same way that he thought his father had made every decision. When one of his decisions failed to work, he lost self-confidence and diminished his power, and he started blaming everyone else. What he came to realize was that he was most powerful when he could confidently admit when he didn't have the answer and open up a dialogue with others to explore options. In this way, they could ultimately co-imagine and co-create an even better solution. By reclaiming his power, he was speaking from a place of leadership (which he actually had all along). Once he reclaimed his rightful power, he started to exude leadership, and it rubbed off. Now the story line changed from "the problem is them" to "the solution is us." Instead of "they are making us lose," it became "we can do this and we will win."

The story shifted. Initially, the president and team looked outside at pressures they could not control. They were lost in the weeds they created for themselves. Each time they pulled up the weeds, the weeds came back. Then the president reclaimed and embraced his inherent power, inspiring others on his team to engage. Together they co-created collective insight and had a breakthrough. They pulled the weeds from their roots with reclaimed power to lead with fresh insight and confidence.

One at a Time

If the solution for each individual is to unlock his or her power, then you are going to have to embrace a personal, sometimes awkward, journey to discover and reclaim your power. This journey is difficult because it forces you outside of your comfort zone. Anytime you go or are pushed past your "edge" of comfort, there is naturally fear and appropriately a sense of risk for where the journey may take you. But we need to find our edge and take a step beyond!

This journey starts by admitting that the status quo no longer works. You have to be willing to change, grow, learn, and take the risks necessary to reclaim your power. Said another way, you have to find your voice again. Whether you had it once before and lost it to a bully boss (who had a louder or stronger voice), or you never used your power (maybe you had it as a kid but left it behind in middle school), the truth is you've always had your voice—you may not have realized it. Maybe something happened to you last year or at the beginning of your career. It's time to take it back. It belongs to you.

You had your voice at one point. You said whatever was on your mind: the good, the bad, and yes—at times—the ugly. Until at some time in the past, you learned that doing so was not a good thing. Maybe your parents didn't like your directness, or a teacher was opposed to you disagreeing, or the cultural belief that "there isn't any room for emotions at work" was firmly implanted. Or maybe you never saw a healthy way of addressing conflict or sensitive conversations. So instead of dealing with conflict in a messy way, you grew to believe it was better to not deal with it at all.

We can over-accommodate our boss, a habit that leads us to "self-govern" our expression. When we wait for the boss's opinion, or in some way hold the belief that it is disrespectful to challenge our boss, we have lost our voice.

This personal journey inward to reclaim your power, your voice, needs three pillars to be successful. Just like any trip that you would set out on, you would have a destination, a map to guide you there, and the resources to make the journey.

The first pillar for the journey is a destination. The destination is hopefully getting clearer—having more of your voice, your personal power, or greater alignment to your purpose, etc. This destination provides the necessary beacon that is calling you to step into your power, and the vision for what that can be when you get there.

We all know the saying, "When the student is ready, the teacher will appear." A guide on the journey is a crucial part of the second pillar of having a map. We can't always see what we need to by ourselves. We all have blind spots that we only see when someone else gives us feedback and support. Sometimes that can be a good friend, a member of the clergy, a coach, a therapist, anybody that can be trusted to speak to you about things that you may not want to hear.

The third pillar of the journey are the resources necessary or, in the case of work, a group to support you with integrating the new behaviors. This can be your team at work, a group of friends that are all a part of an accountability group, or some other form of support group. Change is hard! Accountability and support are crucial to actually integrating the changes that you want in your life in a sustainable way. You will need to leverage the power of the group to make that happen. The third pillar also includes practice and reading to build your understanding and knowledge. These practices become a way to ground you in how you want to operate each and every day. Without these practices, the inertia of the status quo will slip back into the driver's seat of your life. You will default to old patterns and the hard work that you're doing to find your voice will be wasted.

This process can be awkward and difficult at times. It's not as simple as just showing up at work the next day, being vulnerable and transparent with all of your power on the line. You can't just flip a switch. You will need to work through the different layers of risk, self-limiting beliefs, and other forms of resistance to fully reclaim your power.

Growth Mode. Power Is ON!

As each individual joins in, the magnitude of the team's collective power grows at a faster rate. When we take that leap of faith to trust the process, then all of a sudden amazing conversations begin to happen. Life-changing, team-changing, organization-changing connections and engagement occur.

This discovery suggests that every team has the potential to turn itself around and connect at an authentic level, find its hidden and unclaimed power, and come alive through leveraging this power. Once we make this critical shift, everyone becomes a leader, though they lead in a different way. Individual leaders start shining a light on themselves that reflects a broader light back on each other person and the team.

The geometric power of the team emerges as each member brings his or her authentic self to the circle.

The Opposite of Conscious Choice— Unconscious Habits

The shadow message is another way of illustrating how important self-awareness is. In this message, the shadow is a part of you that unconsciously operates in your life anytime you are making choices. In these times, you are operating out of your shadow, as opposed to operating from your light. By shining light on your shadow (or blind spot), you can shift to making conscious choices. With these conscious choices, each individual can now contribute their whole self. Within the team, this creates even more trust and ultimately a keen sense of belonging.

The authenticity allows the team to safely and energetically navigate through any awkwardness that results from their diversity and to positively integrate their differences. What showed up previously as one-sided lectures advocating insular points of view become productive conversation. Team members who used to speak less and wait for consensus to emerge now speak up with less hesitation. The dynamic of the dialogue changes the value of meetings.

While the group previously contained itself to the area of what was known—dealing with facts on the ground and the certainty of experience—now the team is able to step into the unknown. Here lies the mystery of the future, where insight leads to innovation, where collective thought co-creates breakthroughs. This is where the team works together to elegantly dance in the space of complexity to become a powerful team—where growth mode is to the power of n (where n is the number of team members).

The Boss as a Real Leader

When the hierarchal boss understands and embraces this conceptual shift, that boss comes into the true power of their leadership.

When the boss understands, embraces, and models this new way of being, and creates an environment for the discovery to incubate and develop among the others on the team, the shared discovery will help the individuals and the team grow.

The boss (as we've defined her or him) is an individual, too. And, as we suggest, the boss is also a leader. So, the development of the boss in their leadership calls for them to accept that the best way to get stuff done, to be the boss, to be a real leader, is to encourage others to step into their best version of personal leadership. That means you, as a boss, need to accept that you may not always be right, that you may not always know the answer, that you may not even know who does know. You'll also need to accept that it is okay and even sensible (though risky) to move into the unknown, that it is okay to believe that the best outcome is when you can be both the boss and a leader without having to always lead. Embrace the reality that sometimes the highest form of leadership is when you lead from behind by creating the environment for others to claim their power and step in before you.

But the boss starts out like everyone else, needing to go inward and do their work to unlock their power, too! They may have hierarchical power or authority, but they still need to reclaim who they are.

The work the boss has to do to recover their power may look different to other members of the team. It could be that they are already comfortable sharing their opinions and ideas. As the boss, they are ultimately responsible and may be comfortable sharing in order to meet those responsibilities. The boss may have to learn to be curious rather than defensive when someone disagrees with them, to be open to people who express conflict with them, and to having their blinds spots mirrored back to them from team members. The boss will ask for help when they need it and let go of the need to always be right or to always have the answer.

These changes will push the boss out of their comfort zone as well. But this is the work that's necessary. Even if the boss endorses a culture of authenticity, it isn't easy to accomplish.

The boss that is able to let go of these vestiges of old-school management philosophy and embrace authentic leadership is able to unleash all of the synergy and power available to an organization. The boss will still have the final decision. But for most purposes, they are shoulder to shoulder, as a leader with other leaders, aligned around the purpose of the organization and galvanized by authentic relationships and committed to a common goal. There is no pride of authorship for ideas. There is no finger-pointing for challenges or mistakes. There is no backbiting or turf wars for personal motives and siloed performance objectives. There is only the authentic connection through which the synergy from the best of each leader is harnessed and focused, cutting through limiting beliefs, raising the bar of performance, and providing ever-deepening levels of fulfillment for everyone involved.

We occasionally are privileged to witness this amazing transformation. One of our clients, a young CEO of an Internet company, for whom we have facilitated traditional teamwork retreats, invited us to work with the individuals on her leadership team and a couple of other stakeholders to help them create personal whole-life plans. Accustomed to co-creating an annual business plan together, the team embarked on sharing the personal journey of exploring and building plans for their whole life (what we call "life plans")—going well beyond their plans for the business.

The CEO's vision was that if each of the leaders fully mapped out a detailed personal plan, each of them would claim (or reclaim) their power to lead in business and with life. Further, by going through the process together and witnessing each other's best version of their journey forward, they would be able to support each other's INpowerment.

The CEO was instrumental in setting the stage of transparency and authenticity by being vulnerable with her plan. She described the uncertainty about her role in the company going forward, especially as she was moving closer to the role of chairman. She spoke about challenges with relationships and the difficulty her marriage was facing. The struggles in her marriage highlighted her fears around impacting her two teenage children. Subsequently, as each person unveiled their plans for everything in their lives—from their marriages and kids to financial security and failings—the CEO was able to proactively support each person's vision, including the desire for one of the C-suite execs to start his own company. The CEO was open to changing her role from being the conduit for all communication and decision making, to being an enabler of success for the leaders she had assembled. A board member, who had observed many leadership teams in action over the years, was struck by how this team had come together and been able to affirm their synergy, compared to the many other firms he had experienced. The power and energy in the room were palpable.

The CEO authentically participated in the process—not as the boss, but as one of the individual leaders. She inspired the board member/investor to do the same. And, ultimately, she became the best leader she could be by creating the opportunity for her team's individual journeys to unfold without her having to manage the outcome or do anything more than make space for all team members to be themselves. This shift kicked off the best year the team ever had.

This is how the new boss lets others be leaders! Are you ready to be a new boss? Are you ready to be a new leader? As a new leader, you will look inside yourself to unlock the hidden treasures of your power and serve others by inspiring them to discover and explore their individual gifts. You will become a leader of leaders.

CHAPTER 7

Embrace Authenticity: The New Boss Lets Others Be Leaders

· · · · · ·

Get Real. Get Power.

Here are two INpowerment principles:

> **The members of the team will sustain authenticity at the level of the leader.**

> **The HEIGHT of a team's performance compared to its potential is directly related to the DEPTH of connection among its members.**

These principles suggest that authentic connection is the key to maximizing performance of a team or organization, and that every member of the team, including the boss, will need to be open, accepting, and willing to participate in that cultural norm.

Authenticity is the gateway to the power of leadership. This is a new model for how an organization can change the culture of the company.

Eventually everyone, especially the boss, will need to embrace this cultural change as the team prepares to help lead the company. This change can only be integrated into the organization with everyone's participation.

The big idea here goes to the heart of INpowerment. In order to maximize the performance of the organization, each individual needs to show up and step into her or his power. The journey to full power starts with each member becoming real, becoming her or his authentic self and fully open to the known, unseen, and yet to be discovered. This way they are likely to develop bold ideas, clear vision, hindsight, foresight, and constructive and probative feedback.

Though simple, this cultural change is difficult to pull off. Because we're inviting everyone to come to work with their clothes turned inside-out—to reveal not only what they want to show or expect that we want to see, but also the parts of them (hopes and thoughts) that they may be afraid to bring forth. That kind of show-and-tell is awkward, challenging, scary, and even revolutionary. What if it backfires? What if it works?

When you are willing to let go of your self-limiting beliefs about why you need to hide behind your ideas and thoughts, you will open yourself up to the best version of you—the real you, your INpower.

Each individual will show up differently, of course. That's what we're hoping for—diversity. Yet, as each person shows up with authenticity, our similarities and differences will become manifest with attuned clarity, and the power in that dynamic will multiply. The creative breakthrough will come from the product of what we have in common and the hidden message in our differences—it takes all team members to be *real* for this cultural change to have impact.

This creates an opportunity for someone to lead the charge.

The NEW Boss

This is a brave new world for the new boss as they continue to allow themself to be a member of a team of leaders, not THE leader of a team. What once was a scary territory is now life-giving to both the boss and the team. The weight of carrying the burden of having to be right or to be the person with all the ideas and answers is now gone!

The shedding of this burden brings a new freedom for the boss to explore what they may need to focus on differently within the organization. The boss can worry less about what they have to give to their teammates in direction and ideas, and focus more on what they can take away from their teammates (through helping them remove barriers and blocks to their success). They are leading and the boss is engaged in making them the best that they can be in their roles.

This boss is engaged not just professionally in the lives of their team but personally. The boss has a genuine sense of respect and care for each individual they have the privilege to be working with. So the boss invested in them and they are invested back. Together, they are invested in the greater good of elevating each member of the team and achieving the deepest purpose of the organization.

The new leader looks forward to not just sharing the spotlight, but stepping out of it to shine it on their leadership team. The boss is excited to see the team fully embracing their greatness, as the boss leads them from behind. This is the only way for the boss to truly embrace their greatness, not because their job title gives them the authority, but because their leadership team is thriving and willing to follow them anywhere!

Together, in this new way of operating, the new boss and their team are accelerating the synergy and flow of the team's power.

Be an Easy Act to Follow

The best way for a boss to lead is to act as a role model by being authentic in the context of their role as a member of the team.

As a boss, they give open license to the team to actualize their presence by creating a safe place for the group to explore and discover as a team. The boss sets the highest bar in role modeling by actively listening or participating. As a member, the boss connects to their individual humanity by being vulnerable and communicating to others with empathy and understanding. The more leaders are able to challenge themselves to embrace both—showing their strength of courage, taking risks, aiming high, showing their vulnerability, opening their hearts, and revealing their fears—even in the face of seeming at odds, the deeper the team will be and the more it will achieve. Ironically, showing vulnerability actually strengthens the typical display of courage. This also means that the more shallow a team, the less it will achieve.

In our work, we often serve as role models of being authentic to make it easier for others who are unaccustomed to being vulnerable to follow our lead. We embrace our own philosophy by test-driving our practices before we introduce them.

So, without being directive, the boss can lead by example through their role as a member—just by being her or his authentic self. We saw this come to life with the automotive retailer highlighted in Chapter 2 during a three-day retreat. In our typical fashion, we started the retreat by inviting each participant to get present by checking in with what was on their mind and how they were feeling, as we sat in an open circle of chairs.

The CEO (the hierarchal boss) was sitting to my right. I checked in first to model the process, and then signaled to go counterclockwise. The boss—in his role as a participant—spoke vulnerably about his deep, profound fears and the magnitude of his hope that the team would make it out of the recession. He shared that he was afraid of losing the company and the impact this would have on others. He was afraid of disappointing his family and all of the families he had touched through the workforce. He spoke about his worry that one of his bookkeepers, who was suffering from a chronic disease, would lose her health insurance. He began to weep tearfully and said he felt responsible. Then, his energy shifted a bit as he raised his head and spoke to his belief that the company would make it as long as everyone held on to the core purpose of why he started the business—the ideal "that every person matters."

The other team members immediately connected with his fears and were in awe of his ability to also grasp his hope. His authenticity set the stage for all of the content that ultimately cascaded from the minds and hearts of the team. Suddenly, the accounting manager volunteered to help a Marketing VP with a client problem that had been looming for too long, and two coworkers, recently divorced (though neither had known about the other before the retreat), became supports for each other. That check-in exercise inspired the group to move from a circle of coworkers to a team of fellow human beings who deeply felt each other's pains and aspirations. The authentic connections bound them together in a winning belief and spirit for themselves and each other.

The boss began what was a pivotal year of fighting back—not just to survive but ultimately to thrive. The coherence of the team in its full power was birthed from the moment the CEO became human in the eyes and hearts of his teammates. He was easy to follow.

Everyone Embraces . . . Authenticity!

Ultimately, everyone must be IN! When the other members of the team embrace authenticity, they begin to aspire to their potential as leaders.

There is another INpowerment principle that emerges when the team realizes that authenticity, embraced by all, is the key to true power:

**The total power of the team will only be limited
by each individual leader's ability to step into
his or her authentic self!**

This creates a new and interesting growth curve for everyone. There should now be a pressure to "get real" and stay away from the superficial, creating what we call pseudo-community.

Pseudo-community is the place where all groups start and most groups operate. It's a place where meetings are kept to business issues, and after twenty years of working together, team members still don't know anything about their coworkers. Everyone is content coming together as a functional work group and feigning aspirations that arise from time to time so as to create a well-functioning team. As consultants, however, we differentiate that type of pseudo-community from what we consider authentic community.

Before a corporate offsite with the leadership team of a marketing communications firm, we spoke with each team member. During our prep calls, many expressed frustration over a team member who kept to himself and rarely spoke up. They boasted that everyone else was close. Yet, they had made no effort to expressly discuss any of their concerns or opinions with the detached team member or even among themselves. All they did was complain to us. This, we concluded, was a pseudo-community.

At the offsite, all of the team members began to open up, express their issues, and start to understand one another's journey. As they all began to connect with this "negative" team member, they began to see him as someone that had and was still experiencing significant loss in his life. A sense of empathy began to develop in the group. By the end of the retreat, he was completely embraced by the group. They circled the wagons around him to express their support and care. This team was now operating as an authentic community.

At the authentic community stage, everyone begins to see the superficial. When people fall back into old patterns, those patterns will be recognized as such. Teams that succeed on this journey support one another in staying authentic. As soon as one leader begins to shut down, there is a noticeable gap in the team's synergy and flow. So each leader holds themselves accountable by stepping into their discomfort with transparency while supporting the other leaders.

This support can look many different ways. It can be a helpful reminder to one another, or specific points of follow-up for each person. Once the team has had a taste of the power available through authentic connection, the contrast to the old mode of operating is stark. Those who struggle or are unwilling to make the shift to this way of operating will feel the strai-n. They will be pushed by this new operational modality—authenticity—to take the risks necessary to get out of their comfort zone and step into their power, or find their own graceful way to exit the team or company. This is an authentic evolution, because there are those who won't be able to make the journey. And that is perfect! He or she is being authentic by saying, "I don't belong here!" And the team is being authentic by supporting the idea that this person would be happier someplace else.

This is the same choice that a leader must make when the team and/or hierarchical boss is unwilling to embrace an authentic mode of operating. In that scenario, the leader is being authentic by choosing to leave the organization.

In the end, everyone must be IN!

Free to Lead

With everyone on the team working toward showing up fully and authentically, the new boss can actually engage with the team differently. They can focus on creating an environment where each member is free to be a leader, opening up the gateway to maximize the potential of the team's performance.

One of our clients, a CEO who spent most of his time in the field leading the sales organization, was overwhelmed; he had little time to think about strategic growth and was frustrated with his company's sales trajectory. He was reluctant to step away as the de facto sales leader because he believed that revenue would fall. When we worked with the sales leadership team, we observed that team members felt stymied by the boss. Although they wanted to do more, they stepped back so as not to offend him—because when they attempted to step in, they felt rejected, hearing the unspoken message from the boss that he was better than they were.

We encouraged each of the members to express themselves, and invited them to participate in a visioning exercise to articulate the highest and best use of their time and talent. We asked the boss to go last. After he heard from the other team members, he had an insight about himself: he was dedicating most of his time to leading sales because of his fear of stepping up to lead strategic growth, and because of this limited belief, the whole team became stuck. With this revelation, and by accepting that this team wanted to do more and appreciating their hidden and untapped talent, he stepped away from sales, INpowered himself to step up to focus on strategy, and opened the door for others to lead.

Once a boss embodies her own internal power, this new model of INpowerment transforms the organization. The boss frees herself up from having to prove to everyone that she's right all of the time. The boss can make it safe for the one who has the breakthrough idea to come forward, or for the team to figure it out through mastering creative tension, or as appropriate to make the decision by herself. Moreover this opens opportunities for others to lead, and creates space for individual growth. For the organization, the field of opportunity expands with breadth and depth of possibilities. The limitation of the hierarchy has been lifted, and everyone is free to lead.

Here's an INpowerment principle:

The best way for the boss to lead is to move over and invite everyone else to lead by stepping into their power.

Through INpowerment, the boss gives permission to each team member to bring to life the highest and best use of their time and talent. By INpowering each leader to lead, meetings will look and feel different. Previous meetings where the boss was required to bring the agenda and try to facilitate dialogue among the team will give way to each leader bringing content and/or agenda items to co-create the specifics of the agenda. Discussions led by functional heads that typically elicited half-hearted engagement will shift to lively discussions about each other's challenges and opportunities, because team members are connected, care, and are committed to bringing all that they have.

Additionally, they are deeply realigned around the purpose of the organization, allowing them to bring their power for benefit of the greater good. Border skirmishes and territorial behavior give way to embracing feedback and insights from every leader on the team. Concerns brought to each other's attention shift from being taken as personal attacks to being an expression of a mutual commitment to getting better and improving.

The new boss continues to shift focus to this new environment of authenticity. The boss's focus can now shift from being the person with all the answers to ensuring everyone's voice is in the discussion. They now look for places where leaders may be falling into old patterns of quietness or disengagement. Those all signal where efforts need to be focused to understand the resistance.

In fact, one way to consider a key role for the new boss is to create the freedom for each leader to actually be a leader. Historically, that may have been focused on skill development or to encourage the team to keep getting better in their functional areas. While that may still be appropriate, the primary focus day in and day out is for each leader to be INpowered to show up fully and completely with their voice.

When the culture of the company has begun to embrace authenticity, not just in the C-suite, and it's spreading like wildfire throughout the company from the head office to the cubicles and throughout the shop floor, everyone will become comfortable sharing. This is the authenticity that people are starving for . . . and, they will devour it. Now, the real revolution has begun!

CHAPTER 8

Time to Show Up: Start a Cultural Revolution in Your World

· · · · · ·

Shoulder to Shoulder

AS MEMBERS OF the team embrace this new form of authenticity and it begins to flow into the rest of the organization, the culture of the organization will begin to change. This truly is a cultural revolution.

We are explicit to say "revolution" rather than "evolution," because there is no halfway to the transformation that must take place among teams and throughout the organization. To embrace openness and operational transparency calls for fundamental shifts that shock the status quo. The only barrier to this change is fear—fear of failure, fear of inability to adapt to a new culture, and ultimately fear of the unknown. Yet, the unknown is exactly where growth lives and thrives. It is here that the revolution will take hold and deliver a new way of delivering more value to all stakeholders. This cultural revolution invites us to tear down the institutions that built and sustained those walls that were separating us from real human connection.

You can't partially show up in this process—in some ways you've been doing that all along. No, this is a bit like *The Matrix*, in that when you take the red pill, there's no going back. This is what you have to do—PERIOD! It may take you a while to feel like you're completely there, but it is a revolution nonetheless.

In fact, the processes that we use are designed as a disruptive technology for organizational dynamics. There is nothing evolutionary about it. Because of this, we are able to truly accelerate the creation of an authentic community for teams. This has a huge impact on an organization, because we are focused on accelerating the return on your investment in your human capital to create a team that can actually be authentic.

As this cultural revolution takes hold, the boss will continue to find ways to let go of his or her sense of title, and come alongside other leaders. As the boss releases the need to always make sure that people know they are the boss, the other leaders on the management team—and everyone throughout the organization—can actually connect more openly. They will now be able to become more trusting of the motives and intentions of the boss as they demonstrates that, in most ways, they are just another leader that happens to have different responsibilities. And, because the boss has shown that he or she can lead while being one among other leaders, they open up space for the other leaders to emerge in a safe and co-creative way. What unfolds next is a greater capacity for creativity and innovation, and ultimately productivity. The boss no longer has to push their agenda, rather the other leaders on the team will learn to co-create buy-in to align with the agenda.

But leader to leader, you can genuinely connect. Shoulder to shoulder you can genuinely feel mutual strength and support, a growing and deepening sense that we are truly in this together. That sense of each leader having each other's back is a big part of the trust that is created. Leaders can begin to let go of old fears and suspicions that the boss and colleagues are working from more personal motivations. As each leader actually demonstrates their willingness to be vulnerable, open, and supportive, a deepening sense of confidence will emerge. Where they were actually feeling vulnerable by being alone in their role, they are now gaining strength that comes from shared ideas, input, and support.

Buy-IN

Ultimately, each individual has chosen to buy into their power of individual leadership as a member (and leader) on the team. Not as a way to keep a job or please the boss or advance a career. Instead, buy-in from individuals shows they now think as leaders from deeply inside their souls. And, from that place, they know they will perform better and be happier through authentically connecting to themselves and others. As each member of the team shows up and engages more openly and fully, this will create a depth of connection and bond that opens the gateway to greater performance.

Buy-in is more compelling and important than agreement. You can disagree with a final decision and still give your buy-in, because you have expressed your beliefs, opinions, and feelings. It's better than just feigning agreement because of the inevitable decision or vote. Rather than forcing the vote, the ultimate decision is organic, a product of everyone speaking his or her truth until it is clear where the buy-in resides.

Buy-in means that you authentically believe the proposition that you have more power to contribute, and opening up with your real power inside will help you become more fulfilled and the team become more productive. Rather than agree with what someone else is proposing, you come to this insight through your own journey of discovery. And, your ultimate buy-in makes your decision authentic and compelling. The authentic part makes it more likely that you will actualize your real power. The compelling part suggests that the others on your team will really see you and seek a version of the journey for themselves.

It's exciting for us to witness the process coming to life with different team members. We can't even guess who will be the first to show up and buy in. That is likely because the early part of the journey involves soul-searching elements that neither the boss nor we can see, so it's hard to predict where each member is on the quest until the power unfolds in a tangible way through openness and a new depth of sharing.

We facilitated a leadership team retreat for an aggregator of travel sites, a young company started by a serial entrepreneur with a spotty success record. When we began, we invited each member of the team to imagine the best version of themselves as a leader and how that would translate into a more powerful team. There were seven members on the team, including the boss. We wanted them to ultimately co-create a shared vision of how they would work together. The guidelines called for them to create the vision using a combination of cutouts from their choice of dozens of magazines, including *Sports Illustrated, Redbook, People, Smithsonian, Golf Digest*, and *Rolling Stone*, as well as pictures they could draw using stick figures, abstractions, symbols, or metaphor to manifest the details of their vision.

We gave them two hours of solitude for this creative exploration. The retreat venue was late spring in the mountains of North Carolina, so all but one used the outdoors for the assignment. As they sauntered back to our meeting room, we felt a shift in energy, as if the exercise gave them explicit permission to seek and find the deepest parts of their minds and souls for a vision. Sitting in a circle, we took turns sharing the collages of cutout photos and hand-drawn pictures. The team brought them to life through narrative and probative inquiry. Proudly and with poetic vulnerability, from the first to the seventh leader who shared, the emergence of individual power was palpable.

After the last presentation, we put the creative product in the middle of the circle and invited a meandering, non-linear dialogue that continued energetically until the last pause was a clear indication that we were finished. What manifested was a co-created, shared vision of how the team would powerfully collaborate. And, each leader gave an unquestioned buy-in.

Synergy

The growing power inside each individual radiates to create greater power for the team. No longer concerned about hiding something or being shamed, team members can show up in their power as leaders. This is the core of the cultural revolution.

When the team feels a deep level of trust and acceptance for one another, the quality and depth of their dialogue and shared input will create a positive, upward spiral of ideas and discovery, each building on the other.

This is the exponential power factor that we all imagine when we think of a powerful team. Sometimes referred to as group mastermind, this is absolutely the goal—to consciously choose to create a culture that allows for this synergy to be constantly available to the team or organization, as opposed to having it happen by accident.

This is when the hierarchal boss no longer needs to hold up their business card to prove they are the appointed leader. He can just as easily sit back and invite others to take the lead as he can take a huge leap forward as the first in. He becomes a leader through accessing his hidden and unclaimed power—and everyone sees it. And he now serves as the best kind of role model for each and every individual on the team to claim or reclaim his internal power as an individual leader.

Synergy seems to be desired by all but attained by few. Conceptually we all seem to get the notion that the whole needs to be greater than the sum of its parts. But at its core, the root word for synergy is the Greek word *synergos*, which simply means "working together." This indicates that people have stopped coming together as a functional work group and instead are engaged and connected at all levels (emotionally, physically, and spiritually), which allows them to work together in the most effective manner.

There are examples of how synergy has been created in every organization that we've worked with. Let's look at a few specifics that illustrate the point.

One of our clients was in a mature coffee company. The Keurigs and Nespressos of the world were disrupting their traditional business model, and our client was desperately seeking new innovations to spur growth. In this organization, the boss was open to expanding input for new product ideas. He invited outside vendors, clients, and other professionals from organizations that had a long history with the company to join the management team at a strategic offsite. We were able to create a trusting environment with this expanded group using openness and transparency, and created an INcubator to generate new product ideas. The sharing in this environment brought about a number of out-of-the-box opportunities for the company to evaluate that were based on their core competencies, not just based on coffee. For example, they realized that some of their filtering products, noted as the best in the coffee industry, could easily apply to other purification systems (e.g., water, air, and oil).

Another client, a chemical manufacturing and distribution company, was struggling with a largely virtual management team that had operations worldwide. This group had long been a functional work group, coming together occasionally for annual events, but with their primary focus continuing with their functional silos of responsibility. We were able to bring them together in a way to help them see that they, the C-suite executives, were actually a team—in fact, the lead team. Connecting the lead team and their functional teams as equal operating teams had never been considered before. When they realized the power that came from working more closely and transparently together, it changed how they operated, supported, connected, and collaborated.

This leads to another INpowerment principle that deals with synergy:

How well the President/CEO and their management team work together will be reflected in how the whole organization works together.

Creating synergy can help get clarity on strategic direction, especially in the face of underlying crisis. With one of our clients, a service provider to the federal government, the lack of authenticity had led to sugarcoating the challenges within the organization. There were more elephants in the room than management team members! When we were able to create a more authentic team, we dealt with the elephants, and grounded the team in the brutal facts of where the company and its divisions truly were. The synergy created a significant shift in strategic direction that led to the sale of a division and a refocus on the core business.

If things weren't working before, now the synergistic team will be in the best position possible to uncover and address the real challenges and issues that the team faces. All because they each started by owning their individual voice and power, which allowed them to connect authentically.

Most teams don't even know that authentic connection is something they should be focused on. This connection is the key to synergy. This huge cultural shift offers enormous growth potential for the team and the entire organization.

Revolution

The revolution leads to removal of artificial barriers and unnecessary boundaries created by self-limiting beliefs.

If you drive your car with the parking brake engaged, your power and momentum are diminished. It's the same with the potential of human power in the face of self-limiting beliefs. Examples of self-limiting beliefs are:

"I am not good enough."

"The team won't agree with me."

"I'll be laughed out of town."

"They'll never come up with the budget."

"They've never done this before."

"We always do it this way."

"It's too far-fetched."

"What if it doesn't work?"

These internal voices come from the stories we tell ourselves, tainted by years of messages we got from others and from past experiences that produced anxiety and fear. They are real to us, part of our truth, and we will do whatever we need to do to take care of ourselves. We erect barriers and boundaries to protect us from our self-limiting beliefs. We hold back ideas out of fear of rejection (that voice inside you convinces you that you will be the laughingstock of colleagues). We keep constructive feedback to ourselves because of prior experiences with unhealthy confrontation (you tell yourself that if you object, she will resist giving you resources she controls that you desperately need on your project). All of this means we actually do less rather than more with our power—like driving with an engaged parking brake.

The great news is that once you join the revolution, you will free yourself from the weight of these artificial and unnecessary burdens. Each of us has the power to uninvent them.

The revolution invites you to trade in your self-limiting beliefs for a new set of beliefs centered on INpowerment—the belief that you have enormous capacity, and once you tap into that wellspring, you have sourced the strength of your internal power. And, your natural destiny is to lead by sharing it with the others on your team. All that is required is for you to be ALL IN by showing up authentically—disengage the brake and let it rip!

The revolution is on.

FEEL the Difference!

Now your team is feeling the power that authenticity provides. This new connection creates resolutions to core issues that will propel the company into new levels of performance. The individuals on the teams are even more fulfilled in their contribution.

Ultimately, we measure the results of these philosophical shifts quantitatively with data and metrics agreed to in advance. We know we've succeeded when we see the numbers. It's intellectual and easy to prove.

The energy we're referring to is not intellectual; rather it is emotional and soulful. You will know when you have actualized it—when you feel the difference. The revolution creates a different energy field that takes the place of the old environment where we focus on and play to the numbers. While we continue to use the numbers to confirm the successful outcome, we believe that success is much more likely to happen when we focus on the environment that directly impacts the outcome.

Your team will feel the difference! The energy that shows up when connections emerge between leaders feels different. The energy in team meetings will be different—it will FEEL different.

That's not to say there won't be challenges or tension at the meetings or between leaders. That will always be a part of business. But how leaders are committed to engage and connect will change how all of those situations are handled.

The resulting FEELING will be a deep sense of commitment! A commitment to yourself that you're never going back into your shell—you're going to keep showing up with your voice and in your power. There will also be a deep sense of commitment to your teammates through this authentic connection; you have grown to deeply care and respect your colleagues and you are committed to doing what you can to help them succeed and you're supporting them as people.

There will be a new commitment to the boss—you are now fully INpowered to be your best and you can affirm that the boss has not only embraced the cultural shift for the organization, but also joined with you in the journey. You will follow wherever the boss leads. There's also a recommitment to the purpose of the organization—you embrace a deeper appreciation of what the purpose of your organization is and how your personal purpose can align with it. You can see the broader commitment of your teammates to the greater purpose and you are inspired to make that a reality and let it influence all that you can within the organization to be inspired right along with you.

Can you feel the difference in performance?

The different feeling manifests itself in the way colleagues interact. Rather than compete and even sabotage one another in pursuit of attention and credit, coworkers will collaborate and support each other. Rather than hold back their concern or objection for fear of reprisal or rejection, they'll eagerly come forward with enthusiasm and excitement in anticipation of the creative tension that follows. Rather than coming to work with the dread of getting through another day, everyone will anticipate the mystery of the next unknown opportunity that awaits them. At the end of the day, each team member feels he and she is a leader who has made a contribution. And, that feels good throughout the organization.

After a year of turning things around by bringing in new talent (and inviting the graceful departure of others), as well as changing the way folks communicate, connect, and collaborate, a coaching client said to us, "'It feels good."

Then he added, "It was the best year ever. Our sales trajectory is rising. I can't believe how great I feel, and it seems everyone else does, too, like it's in the ether."

The revolution hit, and the right people connected authentically.

The transformation was the logical outcome of the hard-to-explain energy that just felt different. You know it when you feel it!

CHAPTER 9

All INpower:
But Watch Out for Detours

. . . . . .

Journey of Becoming

THE TEAM HAS now enjoyed a taste of how the group can operate differently. A lingering sense of wonderment and awe may be present as you and the group connect with the new potential available. You may have connected with your own truth and power, in a way that was scary and exhilarating at the same time. You are hopeful, but scared to get your hopes too inflated, since this is new and you are unsure how to sustain this way of being. Although you can enjoy a memorable mountaintop experience with the team, you still need to bring it home and make it stick. Expect conscious or unconscious resistance, even from the boss, which can filter down to the rest of the team. So, the hierarchal boss ultimately needs to buy in and take the leadership role to integrate the revolution until the new way of being occurs organically.

You and the team are on a journey. It's still not done, even though there has been a meaningful step into the zone of authenticity. You are no doubt becoming a different team, with access to power in a different way. You, too, are now different, allowing your ideas and thoughts to be shared—letting YOU be seen and known.

Ultimately, for the team to maximize its potential, everyone, including the leader, will need to be INpowered. We have worked with leaders who say, "If you can just get my direct reports to work better as a team, we'll be in good shape!"—as if we have the ability to magically transform (or "fix") the team to alignment. Sorry, but it doesn't work that way. When we asked the boss (our client who is founder and president of a start-up B2B technical services firm in rapid-growth mode) why he resisted actively participating in the work of building the team, he anxiously responded that he was afraid to admit he had struggled with building the team and did not have the answers.

We told him that he needed to shift believing that he has to have all of the answers to instead realizing that when he engages authentically with the team, he and the team will make the best decisions possible. He needed to trust that by making himself open and vulnerable, he'd create real connections that could strengthen and galvanize his team to join forces in powerful ways. He needed to trust the process so much so that he trusted he would be more effective, productive, and helpful to others when he showed vulnerability—even when he's not the smartest guy in the room. He needed to know there is enormous power when everyone shows up together in that same way.

After a two-day intensive with his team, our client told us that opening up to the team about his fears was more difficult for him than taking the risk of starting his business. He was finally able to tell his team that he'd always been afraid of what might happen when he didn't know the answer, and that he resisted moving in certain directions because of this fear. He told them he was even more afraid of asking for help because he didn't want to appear weak. He shared his memory of dropping accounting in college because he struggled with it in the first few weeks, something he now regrets. As the team learned about the background and context of their boss's fears, they were drawn to his power—even more than they had been attracted to his energy when he appeared as if he had all the answers.

Our client felt relieved of the negative energy he had been carrying for years. In that now empty space, he was able to let in the power of being authentic with his team.

This change begins with having faith in the process until you can experience how being vulnerable and being real can radically affect your organization. Then, you will actually believe: authenticity is what leads to power. The magic in that belief is what keeps us coming back to the uncomfortable zone for more—more power, the power that you feel inside, the power that others experience in you, and the power that you and others connect to when you are all engaged in the process. When the hierarchal boss no longer has to use their title and is able to relax into their inner leadership and sense of power, the boss truly becomes a powerful leader. The team is inspired by the humanity, connection, and care of and for everyone in the room; and this is dramatically different from reacting to a motivational speech.

Starting on this journey requires a leap of faith. That leap is about taking risks. Avoiding these risks has kept you dormant and self-contained for too long. But now that you've taken the first risk, and you've witnessed others willing to take the leap with you, you have built a growing, deepening faith and trust that it is the right thing for you and your team.

As you continue to take that leap and trust that faith, you continue to show up, which encourages your teammates to do the same. Everyone is staggering a bit, as if walking again for the first time. You may fall from time to time, but there is no going back to crawling!

Old Threats from the Status Quo

The world from which we came (the old way) continues to tempt us with its comfort food of cubicles, silos, and individual short-term rewards. The boss will be tempted to manage to the numbers and squeak out tangible victories by focusing on immediate opportunities at the expense of bringing the revolution to the next phase. He or she may have intellectually bought in at the mountaintop, but until they become a living example of the new way, the team will easily revert back to old habits.

One of the ways we fall is when we are tripped up by the old way of interacting and connecting. When we give in to momentary fears of showing up, or get swept up in the speed of delivery and minimized interactions, or find ourselves with unsure footing with other members of the organization who haven't experienced this new way of operating, we may revert to how we used to do things.

This deadly comfort zone can kill this new way of being. A comfort zone is anything but comfortable. In fact, it's the place where you've been dying a slow and torturous death. But, it's familiar and a place to retreat to when the landscape is unsure.

Many times, it is much easier for any individual leader to focus on their talents or specific roles, and performing at the highest and best use of skills in getting the job done, often in parallel with others getting their jobs done in a functional workgroup. With heads down, a lot can be accomplished toward reaching goals. And, when the leader needs to interact with others—in those drawn-out meetings or intolerable conference calls—it can seem like a waste of time to everyone, because so much of what happens is not relevant to individuals. After all, we don't really connect—we just get along. It is hard to justify the time invested (or wasted) when the individual could have gotten so much done. Why bother having a meeting when it does not create value?

So silos develop purposefully: individuals look for ways to minimize connection and do what is necessary to remain functional within the workgroup. And, if goals are met, then the workgroup can even be lauded as a winning team. This will remain effective for a while, especially when the individual players are quite talented. The success from being effective may be enough to stall the revolution. After all, in history we find revolutions arising from challenge or crisis. If the business is doing well—or even reasonably well—why rock the boat?

We were faced with this exact scenario with a client in the online high fashion apparel business. On one hand, this client bought in on an academic level to the big idea of individual and team INpowerment, yet on the other hand, her business had enjoyed an admirable success record, so there was a risk of change, and a powerful temptation for the team to fall back on if the journey to authenticity was too difficult. When we finished an offsite on team INpowerment that we held by the ocean, we had a hunch that as the team returned to the big city, the magic of what we'd created would be a challenge to sustain. Leading a group of talented individuals—some of whom were on the creative side, others who were tech geeks, all of whom had their own quirks—and letting them fall back into their silos was a comfortable default for the boss. We learned to never underestimate the force of the status quo when the status quo is working. The opportunity to transform from working as a group to being powerful as a team can be judged a risk not worth taking.

That is, until we get to the core of how the revolution builds. And we need the full strength and power of the revolution in order to overcome the status quo.

The status quo has its own inertia. It has a flow and rhythm, cultural norms and expectations, the way we do things and the things we do not do. Everyone ultimately adapts to the status quo, doing their best to fit in to the model that will create the least amount of conflict and tension.

Unfortunately, this new path requires that you and the team stay ever vigilant for your truth. It encourages and INpowers you and the team to stay on your edge, outside of your comfort zone, where you and the team can access more and more of your power.

When you catch yourself back in the flow of the status quo—staying head-down at your cubicle, limiting your interaction with your silo of operation, minimizing how much you share—know that everyone and every organization struggles with the same challenge. But the difference is that you know what you must do: continue to step outside the comfort zone.

Walls Crumble When Souls Connect

The cultural revolution builds from within the souls of the people, so the structural essence of the organization is the last to be dismantled. What keeps you pushing against this structure and outside of the comfort zone is the taste of authentic connection that you experienced. This is the ultimate elixir, soothing the lonely soul that has been languishing behind the mask of opaqueness. Mostly, it is the hierarchal boss who brings life into the new way of being by bringing soulful energy—together with emotional presence—to match the intellectual message that connecting is important. When the boss goes from just saying the idea to actually living it, the revolution is under way.

This deep desire to openly and honestly connect is a core need for all of us, including the boss. We have just been so disconnected from the truth of our own voice for so long that we've forgotten who we are.

The working silos are embedded in the organization as a default message that good is good enough, and the silos' walls serve as barriers to change. Yet there can be so much more. But the "more" requires hard, real work, especially in the beginning. When you authentically connect, you actually get more power from others so that you can be even more effective in your individual role. In the process, you have received more from others than you could have expected. With job titles, there are associated limits; yet when we drop them, we have also removed artificial boundaries that threaten our inner power as individuals and as teams. Removing these barriers will motivate all to collaborate more rather than retreat back into operating silos. Team members' perspectives will shift from focusing solely on those within their operating silos to appreciating that a true first team is "core-centric," with leadership counterparts who share common vision and purpose. Together, we journey into uncharted territory. In this place of shared discovery we make breakthroughs that no one could have imagined—or achieved—sequestered in their silos.

Let's return to our client in the online fashion business, with her team comprised of creative and tech talent. We had another shot the following year with the team, this time not on the ocean but in the mountains. We called this a retreat, different from the offsite a year earlier. We had a hunch that the boss invited us back because deep down she wanted a revolution but she did not want to start it.

We structured the agenda of the retreat to parallel what the team was experiencing back home. The first part of the day was a group discussion intended to build safety. We structured the exercises with our approach of "go slow to go fast," and the team was coming together, actually enjoying the creative tension emerging from the group work. This led into an emotional exercise that called for some risk taking. We began to sense real connections. Then, we stopped short, and gave them unique journaling assignments to complete on their own, in solitude outdoors in the wilderness adjacent to our lodge.

We mapped out private areas for each of them stocked with raingear, plenty of water, fruit, and nuts. They could not see or hear each other. We did not tell them how long they would be there and we took their electronic devices and watches. We led them there at 1 p.m. and came to retrieve them at 5 p.m. (In debrief, a couple thought they had been there much longer and others thought the time went by quickly.) Through this exercise in solitude, we recreated the silos that represented how they functioned as a workgroup. After an informal supper in silence, we formed a circle and shared the results of their unique assignments.

It became apparent as the third team member read from her journal that their writings were sequential pieces of a larger story that was emerging. They decided to assemble the parts and we invited them to take another crack at building their story—as a team. Their individual contributions were important; yet what was critical was the team giving feedback and adding incremental value to complete a more powerful version of their whole story. The exchanges were becoming more powerful with each interaction, and the story that we concluded with was much different than just putting the pieces in order.

Close to midnight and with the full moon shining above, we debriefed the day's activities, and by the soulful connection that emerged, everyone knew that the walls had crumbled.

When our souls transparently connect with other souls, something magical happens. You begin to be seen and known and accepted for who you are and what your viewpoint offers. Your diversity is embraced, as is everyone else's. This creates a deeper sense of understanding and respect for everyone around us.

There will be a tipping point, when the unsure steps become confident strides. The trust in the process is allowing for greater expansion to everyone in the organization. These strides are powered by a new mantra of cultural openness, allowing the process to circumnavigate the remaining vestiges and structures of the former status quo.

Concentric Power

The big idea driving concentric power is that the best way for the team to become powerful starts with the self-belief that you are powerful at your core and can speak your truth. When you bring that energy to the team, and each other member of the team brings their energies, the team becomes more powerful. As other teams follow, the organization becomes powerful.

It's the difference between a four-by-four relay race and four great runners running the mile in different lanes: the relay team builds on each, drawing more power from each of the runners, while four great runners going the mile at the same time are competing against each other rather than complementing each other. Even when you think you may have reached your limit individually, when you have stretched yourself beyond what you believe is humanly possible, there is always more strength and hidden power residing within the team.

We saw that kind of power come to life at another team retreat we facilitated. A light manufacturing and distribution company had been recently acquired from the original owner and president by private equity investors, who installed a new CEO to take the firm to the next level. The original owner was staying on board for at least another two years, tracking his significant earn-out opportunity. We were asked to work with the leadership team to support the integration of the CEO and transition of the team. There were seven participants, including the original owner (still acting as president) and the new CEO. We engaged each team member in hour-long preparatory calls to get a feel for the landscape. Through the calls, we assessed that the anxiety around uncertainty for the future clouded the concomitant excitement for growth. The former owner was mixed: happy to monetize some wealth, concerned about the value of his earn-out, nervous about reporting to someone younger for the first time in his life, and worried about how he would fit in with his team. The new CEO was frustrated that the private equity firm insisted that we hold the retreat, especially since there was so much work to be done. He had predispositions on the capability of each of the participants and was ready to warehouse the president.

At our first assembly, the unspoken words deafened the silence in the thick air. We knew we had to clear out the truth from the fears, excitement, anger, worry, uncertainty, judgments, predispositions, and self-limiting beliefs. We knew the only way to free energy is to clear the truth that blocks the power inside. So, to clear all the elephants in the room, we patiently and slowly built a safe environment and then challenged, pushed a little, sat in silence, challenged again, until we had a breakthrough. One of the team members began to speak about how she thought she was always better than anyone gave her credit for, how she fought and worked hard in sports and school to get noticed and make a difference, but never felt that she had the opportunity to show it all. As if the water broke in a dam, she let loose with a bounty of stories she was carrying about the team, the original owner, and her first impressions of the new CEO. Her energy was explosive and it ignited others to follow with their stories of the self-talk that was blocking their power. The original owner found his place with newfound power to believe in himself. The new CEO was (pleasantly) surprised and inspired to recognize that he underestimated the team's potential and was curious about what he underestimated about himself. The new team came together from its core—the heart of each member—and with concentric power was ready to bring the energy back to the head office and plant.

Did they bring the power back and sustain it? Not at first.

The new CEO liked the magic that seemed transformative at the retreat. He sent us a warm note of gratitude. He said that he might engage us again the following year, or sometime in the future when it was appropriate. That was a portent. The retreat may have been transformative, but it was not transformative enough that the team fully embraced the revolution. The retreat turned out to be an event, rather than the beginning of a journey. The CEO reverted to his playbook, one that had worked in a turnaround before, the reason the private equity firm brought him in. But this firm didn't need a turnaround; it was a growth opportunity. The team was already filled with underachievers who were beginning to get comfortable with the uncomfortable feeling of expressing their power. He didn't think that the company was broken. The fix was to set the stage and build intentional rhythm around tapping and nurturing the natural flow of power that could cascade from the team and through the organization.

Yet the CEO had a blind spot. Fortunately, one of the board members, whom we worked with on several other engagements, became aware of this and asked us to coach the CEO. Somewhat reluctant at first, he ultimately embraced coaching as a growth opportunity and gained self-awareness around his biggest blind spot: he had always achieved huge success because of his signature strength—being adept and precise at execution. He'd been trained as an engineer, earned his MBA, and rose through the ranks at a large manufacturing firm until he was selected to run a turnaround. Along the way, he was more of an individual performer than a team player.

Success here, however, would need to take a different path; and he had to believe that his greatest power came from his capacity to connect with others, rather than from directing the precise execution of a well-thought-out plan. As the team struggled through two quarters, he admitted that he needed help. We scheduled an ad hoc team offsite, and the CEO uncomfortably yet authentically opened with vulnerability as his persona switched from what had been know-it-all to a humble and curious person. He shared that his success to date had come from a model that would not work here, and he was struggling to figure out how to be the leader that was needed.

He told the team that he always resisted opening up and connecting with others because that would hurt his game face. He wanted to remain sharp and objective. Now, he was realizing that he could actually unleash more of his power when he relaxed into being authentic, being human, and that he could not do it alone. That spark was an invitation for the others (including the original owner who had been relegated to a back seat) to become supporters of the CEO—and ultimately believers in themselves, in their own power. The third quarter blew away the expectations, and by the anniversary of the retreat, the team was ready to celebrate the magic of INpowerment.

This concentric power is at the core of why the goal of being a team has value; that's where the sum is an exponential expression of its parts. What may have been a bit of a push, where you had to push yourself out of your comfort zone and into the zone of authenticity, has now become a pull. Everyone on the team is pulling everyone else into the zone, because that's where the power lies. That's where your best creativity and inspiration exist. That's where your deepest sense of fulfillment comes from in your work. This is where your individual purpose can now thrive, aligned and connected to the core purpose of the organization.

INspiring: Making the Magic Last

This journey is exciting and transformative for the individuals and team. It's also a bit scary, because you WILL be pushed out of your comfort zone. If you are not pushing yourself to your edge, then you are not growing. If the team is not pushing itself to its edge, it's not growing. Then again, you are probably not reading this book because you want to languish in the status quo. This is a journey that will show you how to bring your best talents to the group. When everyone on the team begins to do that, magic happens.

While many leaders and teams have experienced that type of power before, the opportunity is to set the team up to sustain that level of performance on purpose rather than having it occasionally happen by accident.

Even though the magic of INpowerment is best embraced as emotional and soulful connections, in order for each individual and every team to become INpowered, we must set the course with intellectual intentions that lead to clear actions.

There is no silver bullet that creates authenticity! As we've described, it is definitely a journey of becoming. It's a journey, period—there is no real destination. As organizations continue to grow, ever-expanding knowledge is available to the individuals and the team, allowing the group to continue to grow into more and more of its available power.

Creating a culture through a journey of becoming INpowered is counter-intuitive to the classic destination culture from which most businesses operate. The fiscal measurements to track performance on a monthly, quarterly, annual basis establish these destination milestones. Business leaders have been taught how to manage to these destinations. Initially, individuals and teams may feel that a culture of "journey" and "destinations" can't coexist. But we believe that rather than an "either or" dilemma, it is a "both and" opportunity. They both can exist, and the culture of becoming will open up the power to create more effective and fulfilling destination management.

The key to making all of this sustainable is to have very clear, agreed upon intentions and staying committed and accountable to the behavior, motivations, attitudes, and actions necessary to stay on the journey. The status quo is real in every organization. Some environments carry more risk than others. Some individuals may have greater personal journeys necessary to unlock the hidden gold within.

When every member of the team begins to show up with authenticity naturally, you will know that the magic is here to stay. The organic transformation will have changed you and the team forever. One of our clients recently shared that after a team retreat, he has embraced a different purposefulness of connecting authentically when working with his colleagues that has forever changed his perspective of their individual power and of the team. He can't go back.

Every true journey is rarely a straight line. There will be fits and starts. There will be times when expressing ideas and thoughts may get a little messy. Whatever the case may be, it's all good. This is new territory for everyone. We are all committed to seeing this through because we've had the unbelievable taste of what it's like to truly connect! That taste continues to inspire us to do whatever we need to do to stay on the journey.

CHAPTER 10

Hang On: Disruptive Processes Ahead

• • • • • •

Unlocking the Power

A CULTURAL REVOLUTION calls for a dramatic change, or disruption, in our way of being. To get to our infinite store of hidden power inside, we use disruptive processes to unlock it. Although this may sound a bit scary, don't be afraid to be afraid! This is the gateway that we need to go through to get to the power on the other side.

In the context of a team, a disruptive process is by definition doing something that the team wouldn't normally do. It disrupts our normal "business as usual" protocol. This requires getting comfortable being uncomfortable. Once comfortable, it is time again to stretch into the uncomfortable zone. And, keep stretching. Again. Ultimately, it will be comfortable being uncomfortable.

An example of this is how we start meetings. Think of your normal meeting experience. Typically the agenda has been pre-distributed to the attendees. As soon as everyone arrives, you might greet each other. "Hi, how are you?" elicits the rote response of "Great, how are you?"

which then elicits yet another superficial response of "Fine." Then most everyone continues to look at their phones, knocking off emails and texts, even after the meeting has opened, and typically several times during the meeting. The meeting leader will jump into the agenda to push through all of the topics, trying desperately, but rarely able to finish on time, which pushes everyone's meetings, which they have scheduled concurrent to this meeting, back. This starts another long day of never catching up.

Instead of this "business as usual" approach, the way we like to start our meetings is to have everyone turn off all electronics (or in some cases, collect cell phones in a basket when everyone comes in the door). This simple step immediately pushes everyone outside of his or her comfort zone. The eye twitches and technology withdrawals begin! Excuses and rationalizations about why they have to have their phones are endless. Nonetheless, we keep the phones until the meeting is over. To bring your power and engagement to the meeting, you have to be present, not distracted by other matters, and this is all about accessing your own and the team's latent power.

This disruptive practice requires you to be here and present, rather than distracted.

While we believe power is always available for access, we find that many leaders—and ultimately teams—have difficulty finding it. That's because genuine power comes from connecting to authenticity, both inside the individual and with others on the team. Small, incremental steps toward that kind of real connection with others often default back to the status quo of staying in place in silos and functional workgroups.

That's why we need to disrupt the status quo, even if it shocks the system.

By mastering the art of authentic connection through disruptive processes, leaders and teams learn to safely explore and access the hidden and unowned power stored inside themselves to accelerate the manifestation of personal or organizational visions. This will enable a shift from functional workgroups to high-performing teams; from idea paralysis to product innovation breakthroughs; from a stagnant workplace to an elevated company culture.

In the previous story, we spoke about turning off cell phones and electronics. These aren't the only things that keep us from being a high-performing team. Many times, traditional formalities and routines put us into a rote form of operating, often reinforcing a lack of genuine connection, as this next example illustrates.

We were working with a children's playground equipment manufacturer and distributor that relied heavily on independent dealers across the country. Those dealers recognized their dependence on our client. Thus, they created an advisory board comprised of representative dealers and members of the leadership team of the manufacturer to exchange information and ideas; however, both sides—manufacturer and dealers—found the meetings a waste of time. So we were brought in to help diagnose the symptoms and recommend a course of action.

We conducted confidential interviews with each of the advisory board members and found them filled with open and unanswered concerns about each other, pent-up frustrations about what each side saw as inability to change, and—on a positive note—specific ideas about what was required to break through the challenges in the playground market. The problem was lack of real dialogue, even though they had formal quarterly meetings.

We decided to revolutionize the next quarterly meeting. Instead of a boardroom, we met in a living room with no table. Instead of exchanging information through formal reports and PowerPoint presentations, we disrupted these regular practices that were no longer working for them.

We created a safe space for everyone to speak their truth—concerns about manufacturing delays, issues of transparency in pricing, local government regulatory challenges, unanswered questions about real sales data, judgments of backstabbing, feelings of frustration, and fear about losing market share were all out on the floor. It was chaotic for a while, but the conversation stirred up the energy to a place where the common humanity of everyone's emotions, together with the common business interest of selling playground equipment to schools and towns, became the center point of the meeting. Everyone engaged with the power of truth, through which the team was now able to explore the unknown where the magic of discovery led to a breakthrough that ultimately changed the landscape with competition. This resulted in a 9 percent increase in market share over the next six quarters.

Shift from Functional to Performing

As we've suggested, most management teams meet the baseline of how Merriam-Webster defines "team": a group of people who work together. We describe that as a "functional workgroup," where the functional disciplines all gather in a meeting, superficially discuss ideas and exchange data, then return to their functional areas where they perform tasks in isolation. But what we think of when we think of a team is individual leaders coming together in their power to achieve extraordinary results—the type of team that creates the concentric power described in Chapter 9.

But, as often happens, many teams just get by and are complacent with decent results, perhaps even beating its numbers enough of the time to remain under the radar. They're resigned to stay functional as workgroups, cooperating with each other, usually operating in parallel on a need-to-know basis. If it isn't broke, there is nothing to fix. When problems arise, the workgroup can figure it out; but its functionality only goes so far. There can be so much more. But that requires greater authenticity—more skin in the game—to access the hidden power that will lead to transformation of the workgroup into a high-performing team.

So we again unlock the power through disruptive processes.

If we go back to the initial meeting example described previously, the group is already functioning at a lower level than possible because they are constantly distracted by electronics. They are not actually present to engage because they are thinking about the rest of their to-do list. As part of this process, the simple guideline of "no electronics during meetings" creates a small but meaningful mind-shift to help the team stretch outside their comfort zone and create an environment of being present that sets them up for success and improved performance (more guidelines are in Chapter 14—Rules of Engagement).

That choice to stretch was a conscious one. There has to be an intentional choice to shift from the old way of interacting to embracing a new way. A choice that will be difficult at first but is necessary to become a true high-performance team.

Stretching the unused muscle brings the team into the zone of discovery, where being comfortable with not knowing and exploration of the unknown leads to innovation and breakthrough. Playing it safe calls for the team to stay in its comfort zone, where the only questions asked are the ones where the answer is anticipated, where the discussion is narrow. The workgroup gets together to solve problems, and each silo head is expert in their field. So, we contribute the sum of the knowledge we have, yet limit discussion of the areas not known by anyone outside the respective silos of the workgroup, in this way collapsing the potential of the team into this finite area. Thus, the workgroup can effectively function within the limited range of exploration and usually problems are solved in a timely and productive manner. The process then becomes self-perpetuating.

Why change?

Getting to the next level of breadth and depth requires the silos of the workgroup to come together on a co-creative process of exploration and discovery outside their comfort zone. To get there, we need to disrupt the dynamic and challenge each individual to get out of the comfort of the silo, where he is the resident expert, and take the risk of playing together in an unknown place. The good news is you include everything you know and get the benefit of everyone else's knowledge, and everyone is open to the vast and infinite unknown.

Sparked by an inspirational story he heard about the journey of a member of a family business who broke away to become an entrepreneur of a start-up, one of our coaching clients asked us to help him bring that spirit to his family business to enliven a four-decades-old fresh foods distribution company. He did not want to break away; he wanted to break through. This family's company had survived many economic storms and found ways to adapt to the vicissitudes of developments in agribusiness, refrigeration, and transportation. We met individually with the team members, the head of the warehouse, the head of purchasing, the finance head, the head of operations, the head of marketing, and the head of sales—all seasoned, most homegrown, who had touched at least two generations of family leadership. They each knew the drill and were masters of their domains. Speaking with them separately informed us of the rigidity of their discrete silos. To break through them, our intuition was to disrupt the high level of comfort that made them complacent.

Get Comfortable Being Uncomfortable

When it feels uncomfortable, you know you're on the right track. When you get comfortable, you need to remember to get uncomfortable again.

The first level of discomfort we introduced to this team was to change the name and place. They called themselves "the management committee"; we called them "the leadership team." They had always met in the same conference room filled with old pictures of the founder dating back to the '60s—and in some ways, the energy of the great-grandfather seemed to still be directing. So, we met offsite at a meditation center. (We even pushed ourselves outside our comfort zone!)

Even before we started a series of intellectual and then emotional exercises to disrupt the normal rhythm of their everyday activity, the participants were noticeably uncomfortable. Yet each committee member made it through, picking up that the others were similarly impacted and also moving forward.

Our objective was to create an experience that would give them an early victory in discomfort so they would continue to be open to new ideas, to change, and to mixing up the standard rhythm of working as a group.

Once we saw them letting go of the initial anxiety brought about by uncertainty in the unknown, we introduced another disruptive opportunity—this time on point to the way in which the committee was operating. We invited them to speak their truth about whether they believed the way that the founder had organized the committee using practices from the 1960s was the best way to proceed today. We asked them to express their feelings about making changes.

We started that exercise just after lunch, and their high energy continued well past the time slotted for dinner. The longtime committee members spoke about change being akin to betrayal of the company's lore set down by the founder, which gave permission to the current CEO (grandson) to talk about how he was living in the middle of the tension between betrayal of his family by insisting on changing the dynamic and betrayal of his own soul by keeping things in place. The sharing of pent-up emotion and judgments pushed against the safe boundaries of comfort into new levels of depth and connection.

Even though the committee had known each other for years and had been through lean and strong times, they had never connected with this level of transparency before. The committee that had been operating effectively for years in parallel tracks was now acting more like a team—sharing new and bold ideas that brought them to the next level of discomfort.

In our debrief the next morning we had them acknowledge, accept, and appreciate that they had taken a safe journey into the unknown and had safely returned. We replayed how we increased the level of discomfort each time they reached a new level of comfort. They appreciated how far they had come so quickly. We asked them if they wanted more of it when they went back to work. With both anxiety and excitement, there was clear buy-in for taking this new way of being back home. We talked about the difficulty of staying the course alone, and—to our delight but not surprise—they committed to supporting each other on a daily basis with new rhythm for individual and group accountability to openly and strategically co-create the new version of the company. They were starting to take on the attributes of a performing team INpowered through their authentic connection.

This team was definitely uncomfortable. But when you are uncomfortable, you are on an edge. The tension that the team may feel, as individuals are on edges, puts the team into growth mode.

When the team is in a more superficial mode, they are a pseudo-community or in a transactional relationship. This is an appropriate way to connect with 80 percent of the people that you work with or meet in your life. But for those people with whom you want to have a deeper, more authentic connection, you need to push into your discomfort. You need to show up and do things differently, creating chaos.

Take the previous meeting example: simply turning phones off will push the team into chaos. But the goal is what's on the other side of chaos—DISCOVERY! This is where you learn something about yourself and others on the team. The team will also learn and grow together. If we again track this previous example, you may realize, once you stop reacting to not having your phone and accept that you and everyone else will be present, that you actually connect more to everyone in the room.

You may realize you are more connected to yourself, which allows you to participate more fully in the conversation. You may feel like the meeting was more productive and fulfilling, as opposed to typically feeling like it's a waste of time.

When you can get through to discovery, you actually are learning more and more about yourself and others on the team. You will see and understand their motivations more clearly. You will get people's points of view more completely. You will be sharing at a more transparent level. The team is becoming an authentic community. This is where the full power of the team resides.

This leads to another INpowerment principle:

The power of the team is directly related to the authenticity of the team.

Mastering Authentic Connection

When we get to the point where we automatically push ourselves—even without thinking about it—to become uncomfortable, we know that we have mastered authentic connection.

Let's again draw on the previous example of starting a meeting. When the group knowingly drops their phones into the basket at the beginning of the meeting, without griping or complaining—in fact, looking forward to a reprieve from the relentless bombardment of emails, calls, and texts—and they desire to fully engage in the meeting, the group has reached a different level of authentic connection. They are desirous of more transparency and openness, realizing the contrast now between a more superficial level of connection and feeling drained by the inauthenticity previously experienced.

There is a deeper level of trust that continues to open the gateway for more power. You trust yourself to show up more and more as you trust the group to accept your opinions and diversity. Your trust of the group serves to hold the tension and discomfort that comes with truth and chaos; so rather than running away and shutting it down, you and the group embrace the tension to search for the discovery that's waiting on the other side. Embracing uncertainty is never an easy process, but finding comfort in the uncomfortable helps you resist the urge to fight the process.

To master authentic connection, you also have made intentional choices to follow the guidelines and continue to show up more openly. These intentional choices represent the shift from *trying* authenticity to *mastering* authenticity. Since there is no limit to vulnerability, being authentic is a journey of becoming. The best way to monitor progress along the way is to master pushing against the edge of discomfort, or to become increasingly comfortable being uncomfortable to the point where you do so unconsciously. We tell our clients to go home (and to work) and practice. Then, practice it again the next day, and the next . . .

Integration Takes Time

So how did our food distribution team fare in their attempt to master authenticity and become a high-performing team? At first, it was difficult—too difficult, even painful. Back at the office, in old routines, they easily defaulted back to the ways of the past. That said, they did so with awareness that they were having challenges in staying true to what they committed to at the retreat. They could feel the difference between the spirit of collaboration during the retreat and the energy back in their default routine. They just did not know how to balance the requirements of quotidian tasks with the challenges of dramatic change. Unexpectedly, we received a proactive call from one of the participants who asked for help—she was stepping up as a leader to ask for support about how to continue the revolution we'd started at the retreat.

Here's what we told her:

There is no substitute for embracing the art of authentic connection by practicing being open, vulnerable, and truthful—especially when it's awkward and difficult—until you become the real you naturally. Although any individual can practice alone (and many of our clients come to us because they're struggling with connection in commercial settings), working together on this mastery is a welcome gift. When the whole team recognizes and appreciates the difference in its team power through their connections, members can use each other to practice and work through real-time challenges of chaos, turning them into opportunities to connect and explore. As each team member joins in, the team's energy resonates authenticity. And with awareness of the power in each successive experience, you build the muscle to continue and ultimately become masters.

The team member who called us embodied that message at the next team meeting; she became the first master among masters of authenticity.

A New Normal

The best way to avoid the default is to change it—make a new normal. The old default was characterized by a lack of genuine connection with leaders showing up more as a functional workgroup rather than leveraging the power of the team. Issues and ideas weren't addressed or debated openly, which led to meetings that felt like a waste of time.

In the new normal, people show up with their opinions and ideas. Issues are addressed. Safety is created so people are present, not distracted. The meetings bring an opportunity to create synergy of collective thought, alignment, and commitment for the priorities of the group. Everyone is fulfilled because everyone is in his or her power.

When each member and each team keeps challenging and pushing, we have created a new normal. When elements of the old status quo leak in, then any and all team members address it immediately and quash it.

When every team member knows how to access disruptive tools to help being open and transparent a little less difficult, the new way of being becomes the new normal. At this point, the cultural shift is no longer revolutionary, because everyone is in.

Take the group that has now embraced dropping their phones into a basket. If one member happens to forget and his/her phone buzzes during the meeting, they will be playfully chided by the team for their lapse back into the old way, and reminded to drop their phone into the basket.

This new normal is a bit like a seedling. It will need constant attention to nurture and protect it until its roots are deeper and stronger. That will come from the vigilance of the group. Everyone in this new normal takes responsibility to nurture the seedling. That's because we are all leaders! It's not just up to the boss to nurture the seedling. It's your power. It's the team's power! This is the opportunity for everyone to be engaged. In fact, that's the key to the new normal in the first place: everyone is present and engaged, bringing all that they have to share. That's true on the content side for the business issues at hand, but also on the process side that ensures the new normal is protected.

Operating with disruptive processes is at the core of the revolution. Once you embrace these tools for a period of time, they will no longer be considered disruptive—they are the new normal.

Again, proof that you have embraced the new normal is manifest when the old ways creep in and a random coworker steps in to stop the leak. Back in the early 1990s when offices were becoming non-smoking, many business leaders never thought they'd be able to transition workers into a non-smoking workforce. How could they change default behaviors of a significant group of workers? Although legislation forced business to embrace non-smoking environments, ultimately everyone embraced the revolution as a new normal. And, today, if someone sniffs the scent of cigarette smoke, a worker will immediately step in and stamp it out. It works the same way with authenticity; when there is a sign of someone holding back or taking the easy road, a random coworker will remind the rogue and keep him from slipping.

Our client's food distribution company is still family owned. The management committee now is called "The Team of Leaders." A few new faces (who know only the new normal) replaced a few who (unable to join the revolution) retired. The new product lines that emerged from collaboration will soon be the primary revenue producers. Huge growth has come from a new business development area of expanding restaurant chains. The team continues to challenge itself by venturing inside the area of the unknown where they are comfortable being uncomfortable— their new normal.

CHAPTER 11

Warm Up: Access Power through Vulnerability— Ask, Don't Tell

· · · · · ·

Ask, Don't Tell

IT'S TIME FOR a meeting or offsite, and the team wants to prepare for the big event. There's a lot to cover and you have your ideas about what you'd like to say. Yet at the same time, you're reserved and unsure whether it's worth the risk to speak up. You'd like the interactions to be authentic and therefore productive. So, how do you get ready?

The process calls for taking risks and vulnerability. We begin the journey to authentic connection by deeply listening to what is needed to help make this team thrive. When we work with management teams, we use a questionnaire tailored to the group that helps provide us with data to appreciate the context for where the team is today. Once we have that information, we follow up with interviews to supplement our understanding of what cultural shifts and changes in management meetings and rhythm need to happen, clearing of "elephants" that may be in the room, and sensitive conversations that need to be facilitated. Only then can we begin to craft an agenda that will take the group to where it needs to go.

As you begin your journey of INpowerment, start with that deep inquiry into a vulnerable place.

The INpowerment principle that applies here is:

**Your depth of connection with the team will
mirror the depth of your connection with yourself.**

Before a competitive game, an athlete will find quiet space to visualize the competition, and then stretch his body, do some light exercise, and practice the basics. With a commercial team getting into their authentic power, we encourage each member to get centered inside him or herself. Start centering through getting present in the moment by checking in mentally, emotionally, physically, and soulfully.

Where are you right now—in your head?

You could be focused or distracted, or processing to get present.

Where are you right now—in your heart?

Check in with your full range of feelings, using as a guide the primary emotions of glad, sad, mad, scared, or ashamed.

Where are you right now—in your body?

Is your body humming on all cylinders, or are you aching? Where? Notice the message from inside your body—it can impact your capacity to stay present, and being aware of it will help you focus.

Where are you—in your soul?

This is the wild card. For some, it is their source of strength. For many, it is how you connect (or may be out of connection) with something bigger outside yourself. (We will discuss in detail the check-in process in Chapter 13.)

Before you can connect with the team, first connect with yourself. For example, if you are swimming in a sea of overwhelm, constantly overbooked or stressed about being behind, then you will most likely be totally disconnected from yourself. How could you be grounded and centered—who's got time for that? And if you are completely disconnected from yourself, how can you possibly connect openly and authentically with others? You can't! That's the point: you must connect with yourself first in order to connect with others. That's the new awareness and learning here. That's where the shift has to be made.

Yet, this is where the rub comes in: you have so much to do that the thought of stopping to take a few minutes to do anything that doesn't feel productive for the day's to-do list seems impossible, desperately unproductive, or a waste of time. You probably fear that any unproductive time would just allow more things to make their way onto your to-do list, faster than you can complete them.

So, there is a risk in taking time to ground—it will limit what you can accomplish. Said another way, taking time to BE will reduce your ability to DO.

But what actually happens is that you will become *more* productive, rather than less. So while you may put less time in, you will have more of your power online—power of creativity, analysis, connection, and ability to create synergy with your team. All of these things happen because you have stopped for a moment.

In most activities that we do, we first think about situations or people or activities outside of ourselves to focus on. That's completely normal. But it's also part of the problem. If the goal is to INpower yourself, you start by looking inward. As the Greek sages advised, "Know thyself."

So, invite yourself inside and probe until you find your presence, the gateway to your power.

What's Going on INside

Now that you've checked in with yourself to help get presence of mind, heart, body, and soul, continue to open up by going further inside with curiosity.

First, ask yourself about "you." Do you have limiting beliefs you're holding toward the team or any individuals? What issues do you have with other teammates that are preventing you from engaging more fully? Often, leaders limit the power of the team by the stories they make up about the team's deficits and the impact of what cannot be achieved (these easily become self-fulfilling prophecies). What is the range of emotions that get triggered when you reflect on your role in relation to the team? This will inform you about how to navigate frustration or anxiety around certain individuals.

Next, how do you feel about team or organizational challenges or blind spots? Invite yourself to diagnose these flaws that might be getting in the way of the team becoming more powerful. What are the organizational challenges that emerge from those blind spots or other stumbling blocks? Do you see blocks to achieving the results you're committed to? You are getting clarity on what is most important for you and the team to tackle.

We've worked with a profitable firm that manufactures and distributes commodity products, which historically stood out due to its outstanding customer service and pricing. The firm also held a long-standing self-limiting belief that they couldn't create and market innovative or specialized products that would earn a higher profit margin. And, whenever the idea was raised, it was surely shot down. Eventually, no one even raised the idea; it was deemed a waste of time and embarrassing. Because of margins tightening due to competitive pressure, we were invited to help the team explore options. At an offsite, we introduced an exercise that called for each team member to write down five self-limiting beliefs they held around what they could not safely bring to the team. We designed it as a secret ballot so no one would hold back. Not surprising to us, the number one response was "the inability to raise the opportunity to venture outside of commodities," and the corresponding emotion was frustration. Just getting this on the table was enough for the team to start exploring the blue-sky possibilities of research and development and the minor retooling of the plant to support a specialty product. That's the course the firm has taken.

In another example, we were asked to work with a family-owned medical instruments distributor. The CEO brought us in because he was struggling with getting his management team aligned. Although they had brought in an outside consultant for a strategic planning process, the team still didn't seem to be completely aligned with where they were headed.

After reviewing the questionnaires and conducting interviews with everyone on the team, it was clear that everyone was doing their own thing, in part because there was a lack of connection and understanding about what others on the team were doing, their perspectives on strategy, and even their backgrounds, though many had worked together for over five years. They were swamped with activity because the CEO was hyper-focused on growth and was constantly pushing the group. And, the CEO had made a controversial choice with the new CFO, promoting a controller from within that was relatively new to the company, and the VP of HR who was also green. Many of the team judged these decisions as efforts to minimize costs at the expense of experience and quality. The CEO was also traveling extensively for both personal and professional reasons, so access to him was limited.

After learning all of this, we realized they were not comfortable sharing their concerns or openly bringing ideas to the group for debate and alignment before decisions were made. There had also been no attempts to onboard the two new members of the management team, so they were not yet integrated into the management team. It was also evident that there was little safety or trust to share these concerns. The lack of onboarding for the new teammates distanced them. The CEO's lack of availability and transparency exacerbated the group's uncertainty about his motives and the context for his decisions, which ultimately undermined their commitment to the strategic plans.

What they needed was a process to build trust to onboard the CFO and VP of HR, and create safety with the entire group, so that real issues and concerns could be addressed. That process would lead them to ultimately reaffirm the direction and commitment to the strategic and tactical priorities.

So we planned a two-day offsite. We chose a beachside resort for the offsite and knew we were going to have to get the company present and connected with themselves first, so that we could get into some of the other challenges. We started the meeting by asking everyone to go for a thirty-minute walk outside in solitude and silence. We gave them each a journal and asked them to reflect on the questions, "What do you most want for yourself and the group from this offsite? At the end of these two days, what do you want to be leaving with for yourself? The group?"

Their anxious looks at one another were priceless, yet they ultimately found their way outside for the exercise. When they came in, we asked them to share what they came up with. Their clarity was on point! Each person was engaged and focused.

We then had them speak to the strategic plan from the point of view of their functional area. They shared their primary strategies, goals, and key initiatives, all of which led to meaningful discussions.

We then asked each of them to journal: 1) What are your self-limiting beliefs about your ability to achieve your areas of responsibility? 2) What are your self-limiting beliefs about the ability for this team to deliver on the strategic plan?

What happened next was truly incredible. We started with their personal self-limiting beliefs. The CEO began by saying that he struggled with confidence issues, and was always second-guessing whether or not he was worthy of the CEO role or just lucky because he was a member of the founding family. He was worried that he couldn't mentor people on his team the way they needed to be mentored, and he was scared of letting his team down. Because of these worries, he stayed on the road to try to help create new strategic partnerships and networks that could help the company in the future, rather than micromanage in a way that might screw things up. Everyone's jaw dropped! You could feel the compassion in the room grow as his raw honesty was expressed. The CEO's transparency created a model for the group! Everyone that followed was extremely open and transparent. Both the CFO and the VP of HR spoke to their fears that they lacked the experience necessary to really give the team what it needed. The COO and VP of Sales & Marketing were also deeply vulnerable and real about their self-limiting beliefs.

All of this openness led to a discussion about how the team could interact and support one another differently to help each person overcome their self-limiting beliefs. We provided the group with a model on how to shift those self-limiting beliefs and create new INpowerment beliefs.

We then discussed self-limiting beliefs about the group. This was another completely transparent conversation. All of the concerns poured out: the lack of understanding or motivation of the other team members; the CEO's lack of availability; poor communication within the team; concerns about the CFO and VP of HR's experiences; the history of the family patriarch and founder occasionally showing up and redirecting the team.

When you get clarity about what is going on with you, then you can sort through what you most want and need for you and the team to achieve.

What You Want

When you have connected to yourself first, and then fully and transparently connected with your group, you have opened the gateway to make direct requests about what you want. Start by looking inward to get clarity up front about what is important to you. Explore what you want to have happen at the meeting, or what a successful outcome looks like if you get what you want.

Step into your sovereignty. You're the king or queen for the day and can ask for what you want. Although you may not get it, if you don't start by asking yourself what you want, you'll never know.

We've seen many individuals on teams wait for someone else to tell them what to do or defer to the boss's wants. After all, these actions are less risky. Yet, if everyone does this, we're severely limiting our potential. All of the ideas left on the table go to waste. So, when it's safe enough to share, then we invite all that power to thrive.

It's our custom to conduct pre-offsite interviews with each participant. Our favorite question is, "What do you want to have happen at the offsite?" Although we're thoroughly briefed in advance and are often given parameters by the sponsor or boss, we still invite participants to speak to their most sovereign wants. The outcome of those conversations often dramatically changes the theme for the offsite or shifts the emphasis. In our conversations, the participant is breaking the ice, and warming up to speak their truth in a confidential, safe manner.

To paraphrase one of the great philosophers of our time (Mick Jagger): You don't always get what you want, but you might just get what you need! We have to INpower ourselves to ask. To take a risk and not get what we want. To risk our want going unfulfilled, or risk being hurt or let down. But when we have an authentic community, we're less likely to take these situations personally, because we have connected more genuinely, have built a real sense of trust, and have become aligned around the shared purpose of the team and organization.

If a decision doesn't go the way you wanted, it could mean that's what's best for the team. As long as you've had your voice in the discussion and openly contributed to the debate, you're satisfied with the outcome and ready to support it going forward.

We were working with an entrepreneurial start-up that was focused on distributing educational software in Latin America. Every member of the team was working crazy hours to get the company off the ground and generate positive cash flow. The new CFO was relocated to join the company. She was single, and her dog was her best friend in the world.

We led a corporate offsite to kick off the New Year and prioritize tactical initiatives. Once we established safety and had everyone connected, we invited everyone to check in and tell the group what was working for them and what wasn't working for them. After many open comments, the CFO was able to muster her courage and share that getting home late at night every night, only to find piles of dog poop, wasn't working for her. She was feeling guilty for not taking better care of her dog, but was committed to the team goals and objectives and didn't want to send the message that she wasn't dedicated by leaving earlier to take care of her dog. Her ask was to be able to leave at 6:00. She was happy to continue working from home, but was really struggling with the current situation. The team allowed her to do so. She was thrilled. She ultimately was able to find a dog walker that gave her flexibility to stay at the office when necessary. It worked perfectly. That wouldn't have happened if she'd been unclear about what she wanted and failed to ask for it.

As the team discussions unfold, continue to explore what you want to have happen. It's a question that you need to keep asking: what would a successful outcome look like if you get what you want? Is there even more?

Getting Clear and Aligned so You Can Show Up

Getting clarity helps you to be authentic with yourself. This is the key to having a deeper sense of fulfillment and peace. In fact, most of the angst that we deal with internally comes from being out of alignment with ourselves: our beliefs, our values, our desires, and our wants. You can't get to that point of integrity until you've gotten clear, for yourself.

Think about your role on the team as being a "fiduciary" with the responsibility to show up with what you see, feel, understand, and question. This is why you are working in this company. You have chosen to work for the company and bring your talents and gifts to the table. If you don't, if you withhold your contribution in some way, you not only are out of sync with yourself, but with your fiduciary responsibility to the team.

We want you to feel the sense of responsibility, first to yourself, then to the team and organization, to bring your power and voice to the table.

When you have explored and processed what's going on inside you when you relate to the team, and how you see the interactions within the team, you are in a centered place ready to access your power.

You've successfully warmed up and are game-ready. Imagine when each of the other players on your team invests in this intentional practice. Each of you takes responsibility to show up in a centered and powerful way to begin the conversation. As a result, you—and each of the others—have made it safer to take the next step IN.

CHAPTER 12

Taking the Leap: Safety Belts, Please!

· · · · · ·

Where Are the Land Mines? Telling the Truth about How Much Truth to Tell

AS WE'VE DESCRIBED with the stories of groups that we've worked with, each situation, team, and leader will have their own particular challenges. In every situation, we have to determine the best way to approach the group or leader.

This is true for you too. You will need to think about your situation and team and consider how you can begin to show up and be more vulnerable. There are likely risks involved. Those risks are neither easy nor to be taken lightly. What issues do you want to address? How do you anticipate the group will react? Who are you most concerned will judge you in some way or feel threatened by your views?

These are all common reactions that can create some anxiety for you as you think about presenting to the group more of you—your thoughts, ideas, concerns, and wants. These are reactions to risks that you feel. We all have an internal risk manager. Essentially, there is a part of us that is constantly scanning for threats to where we might be at risk for getting hurt. You may recognize it as the internal voice in your head that says, "You better not do this because that could happen and that would be bad."

These risk managers are very good at trying to protect us. But many times, the threat profile they are working with would likely have been created when you were very young and were first hurt in some way. So the situations that can hurt an adolescent, and the depth of such hurt, are different from what you'd experience as the adult you are today.

The child's risk manager matures through the years to embrace the challenges and need of the adult. So it's appropriate to work with your risk manager and assess where the risks are. In your mind, ask yourself the question, "What's at risk for me to show up with my true self at the next meeting?" Notice what your mind replies. The response is from your internal risk manager. This is how you can work with that part of you. You can then look at each of the risks and determine how you would mitigate them and, most importantly, if you are willing to take the risk.

This internal survey of the land mines will help you to navigate that terrain effectively and safely. And, when you consciously evaluate the risks and then make the decision on how you proceed, YOU are making the decisions about when and how you (NOT your risk manager) will show up. Without this conscious evaluation, your risk manager will unconsciously keep you protected by governing your input and your power.

Plot a Course: 10 Percent Stretch

Thinking about risk can paralyze you from stepping into a vulnerable place, especially when you are looking ahead at the worst-case scenario. You may imagine that you'll be fired, alone, and helpless. So instead, imagine that there is a continuum of risk, on one end of the spectrum is where you shut down completely, and at the other end you are wide open. You stand somewhere along that continuum as you subjectively determine what's what. That's your spot of safety, where your internal risk manager allows you to play.

What needs to happen for you to be willing to take the first step? Not the whole distance to the goal line, only a first down.

You'll need to get permission from your internal risk manager to take a small step, say to stretch just 10 percent, in showing vulnerability.

Here's an example of a little movement going a long way. Our client, a private equity firm, recruited a new CEO to lead one of its portfolio companies, a manufacturing company. The new CEO was a seasoned business technologist with a success record of leading growth in relatively short time frames. He was taking over for the founder who sold his interest in the company. The founder was a passionate entrepreneur who had treated his team like family. While the senior management team was sad to see their founder retire, they received significant options from the private equity firm to help retain them.

The new CEO presented his bold strategic plan for growth and went about implementing it in his directive style, a style that had worked well for him in the past. A quarter into his tenure, we received a call from the lead partner at the private equity firm. The performance metrics were off and one of the management team members had reached out to the partner complaining that the new CEO wasn't connecting with the team. We were asked to identify the source of the problem, so we interviewed the new CEO. He was trained as an electrical engineer and leveraged those skills as his primary core competency. He scored low on empathy in his 360 surveys, the polar opposite of his predecessor. In the past, he had received coaching to help him connect with team members on a human level, though he had not yet made progress; until now, that deficit had not hampered his success record. The CEO was very self-aware but stuck on how to change his default of being a lone ranger. We then interviewed the other team members and learned that while they deeply respected the new CEO's strategic posture and ability to harness the resources for growth, they viewed him as a hired gun (not part of their "family") who was brought in for a brief period. In part, they were correct; however, they missed the opportunity to openly welcome and integrate him into their family.

We suggested holding a half-day offsite and barbecue. In that informal setting, we created a physical representation of a line or spectrum of risk (or vulnerability) using a long rope on the ground between two trees—one tree was marked "open and vulnerable" and the other tree was marked "limited vulnerability." We asked each team member, one by one, to stand along the spectrum where they self-assessed their vulnerability with the team to be. We stressed that they were speaking with their feet—no words required. Each of them did, and to no surprise, the CEO was standing close to the far end of the "limited" side.

Watching him stand there alone invited some empathy from the others, and we could feel the CEO reading that energy. Next, we asked them to take turns returning to their spot on the rope, and this time we invited each member to take a small step, a movement of 10 percent along the rope toward openness, and to share something personal about how they were feeling around the current team dynamic. We asked the team member who had the longest tenure to go first, and he spoke about how he had a mixed feeling of pride in how far the team had come, and sadness that it was now such a different and professional, structured business. We then invited the CEO up. He talked about how he had spent his whole life wishing that others would like him for being a regular guy, but he never had figured out how to fit in, so he was driven to prove himself successful by over-achieving on his own. And now, he realized that he needed the team to be successful—and he could not do that alone.

A small step in sharing his honest feelings in a vulnerable way opened the door for the team to truly welcome him as a regular guy as well as their new CEO. During a break, the head of technology made a point to find a private space to let us know that this experience had shifted his perspective of the CEO. He said, "I am now rooting for him to succeed, I actually like him more, and I'll bend over backwards to do my part."

Safety? There's a Novel Idea

When you begin to think about revealing more of yourself and showing up more transparently and vulnerably, it can be a scary thought. But fear is just an emotion, albeit an important one. Think about times that you've been scared. What did you most need at that moment? What did your fear need for you to move forward?

Safety!

If you are standing in the middle of a train track and a train is approaching, hopefully your fear will get you to move off the track and to a safe distance away. This fear is a good thing! And in this example, you have complete control over your actions and safety.

But when you are part of a team, obviously there are others that you will have to rely on to help create trust and safety. Imagine that you are considering a bungee jump off of a bridge that's several hundred feet above the canyon floor. What is the first thing you're going to do? Look at the company's safety record. Then you'll check the maintenance procedures for the safety harness and bungee rope that is supposed to hold you. If you deem it to be safe, and therefore that you can TRUST it, then you'll take the leap.

Taking a risk in a relationship with a colleague requires the same thing—safety. If you don't believe it's safe enough for you to share your opinions, you are not going to. Yet because you have clarity about what you want, you can now navigate the relational and team dynamics to ensure that you express yourself more fully. Because you have clarity about your need to create safety, it's already safer.

Think about your personal relationships for a moment. How many times are difficult conversations avoided because of fear that the conversation may or will upset or hurt the other person? Or we may avoid it because we are afraid that it might even end the relationship. Or we may determine that because the relationship is stressed at the moment, that now is not a good time to address the issue (it's not safe), and we'll wait for the relationship to be in a good place before stepping into a dicey conversation.

This is how our internal risk manager is trying to help us navigate the land mines in our personal relationships. We have to do the same in our professional relationships. However, in order to have tough conversations at work, we need to understand safety.

Safety is not a concept taught in most business schools. This is a new school of thought for businesses to wrap their arms around. Even with the increased importance of emotional intelligence in business, the process of how to share your emotional intelligence hasn't been identified—until now.

Think about these five levels of sharing:

1. Cliché
This is the way most people communicate. How are you? Great! How's the family? Good! Beautiful day today! Yes it is! Easy. Thoughtless. Unrevealing.

2. Current Events
This is also low-risk conversation. Here we can talk about sports, travel, vacation, movies, music, and the latest headline news. These are easy to talk about because there is very little personal sharing.

3. Update
This is describing what activities you are currently involved in. The classic "How was your day?" question gets answered. But again, many times

this is a way to get filled in on WHAT you've been doing, not about HOW you are doing. These are more of a series of headlines of your life.

4. Feelings

These are the emotions that are currently present. Now we are getting into risky territory. To share my emotions would be to make myself vulnerable. Emotional intelligence helps me to discern what emotion I'm feeling in the moment. Emotional intelligence, however, doesn't tell me how to share those feelings with others. In fact, most leaders don't really understand why emotional intelligence would be important to develop, because they don't understand how it can be used on a daily basis.

5. Feelings about persons, teams, reactions to your ideas, etc.

This is the most vulnerable form of sharing. When I begin to reveal my feelings toward another person or team or respond to an idea or even a criticism, I'm making myself the most vulnerable because I'm creating the greatest risk of having others judge me.

Most of our traditional business conversations are focused on the first three levels of sharing. Look at your business meetings. We commonly come together in the conference room where we share a few pleasantries (cliché and current events). Then the content of our meetings is focused on updates of our past week and the priorities for the coming week. That's where we spend our time.

If we are going to be in our power, we have to step into levels 4 and 5. So, you will need to assess the risks and find a safe way to step into those levels of discussion.

You may determine that the risk is too great to share openly with the entire team at first. So, you may start by sharing your thoughts with individuals whom you trust on the team as a sounding board, before bringing your thoughts to the whole team. That can help you to get their feedback and input on how to approach the team in a way that can give you more confidence in taking the risk with the larger group.

Knowing that you have an ally in the room always helps to create safety and reduce the risk.

You may have already been following this approach as an unconscious way to create safety for yourself. The good news is that there is a very conscious, straightforward, step-by-step process to create safety.

Show Me the Way Home: Buy into the Process for Safety

Creating safety in the team is the prerequisite for taking risks. There are five steps to the process of creating a safe space.

1. Getting present

First, getting present in the moment invites you to set aside distractions that will inhibit your power. Your presence leads to your power. We use our energy model to get present by checking in mentally (where are you in your head or intellectually—are you focused or distracted?); emotionally (in your heart or feelings—what range of emotions are you feeling right now?); physically (where are you in your body—are you tired, hungry, alive, fit, aching?); and spiritually (where are you in your soul or in relation to something bigger than you? [See "Focus: Check In with MEPS" in Chapter 13]).

2. Understanding and committing to guidelines and a protocol for how we are going to connect

Next, we introduce guidelines for everyone to embrace as a framework for interacting with and connecting to each other. As examples, everyone commits to speaking their truth, owning their judgments and feelings, actively listening, and speaking respectfully without blaming or shaming. Each guideline provides a safe road for healthy interaction (see the guidelines in Chapter 14).

3. Using the "Clearing and Resolution Model"

We offer a model for everyone to navigate through the unspoken tension and conflict that undoubtedly arise when people work together. Instead of ignoring the elephants in the room, however small, we clear them out so everyone can be aligned with themselves and the people they work with.

The construct for clearing issues uses the following elements:

- Facts—predicate data that can be proven and is not disputed

- Judgments—opinions or beliefs, the story that you tell yourself about the issue

- Emotions—feelings that are triggered by the issue

- Role or responsibility—your part in attracting this issue to you at this time; the particular sensitivity that may contribute to the intensity of emotions or judgments

- Specific wants—desires that may lead to resolution or closure

After the person goes through the five steps, the other person mirrors back the essence of what they just heard so the person clearing knows that they've been understood. Once you clear, it is safe to move to the substance of the meeting (see "Five-Step Clearing Process" in Chapter 15).

4. Completing exercises to take steps toward authenticity

We break the ice with an exercise that invites everyone to practice being authentic. Sometimes this may be a simple prompt that calls for self-reflection and vulnerability. For example, we ask everyone to share an experience from the past month that inspired his or her passion. The question gives everyone a chance to shift from being in their heads to opening up emotionally and soulfully so they become more present with more of their power.

5. Anchoring and integrating the process

Finally, we keep things safe by making sure that we anchor and integrate everything that occurred during the meeting. Before the end of the meeting, we take time to debrief the outputs and next steps to assure that the decisions, insights, and learning can be brought to life in a meaningful way. That makes it safe for the team the next time it comes together.

Intentional Commitment

Now that you are armed with more clarity about the risks that you have to navigate to create safety, the rest is up to you. You are in control of your own destiny. You have to summon your courage and take the risks that open up the gateway to your true power.

Many times this is not a default position. In fact, we've discussed at length how most of our default positions are guarded and invulnerable. So, becoming more transparent and vulnerable is like building a new muscle—the more you work at it, the stronger it becomes.

Following the muscle analogy, if you want to get into shape, you may need to get to the gym to workout consistently. You will have to create a new habit. That will take discipline on your part. Once you've created the habit, the habit will take over and get you the workouts you need.

This is the same with showing up and taking risks. The discipline in this case is intentional. You have to be very intentional because it's not a habit yet. You have to put that at the top of your to-do list every day. You have to be very intentional each and every day to show up. This is also a commitment. You are committed to embracing all of your power and to showing up as your fullest self. You are committed to actively participating in creating a true team, which requires you to be fully INpowered.

These same intentions and commitments apply both to you and the team. The INtegration steps will need constant intentionality and focus as well as a commitment from the team. It is too easy to slip back into the old status quo.

But remember that you can't control anybody else on the team but yourself! This leads to another INpowerment principle:

**The only person whose authentic engagement
you have full control over is you.**

CHAPTER 13

Where Are You Right Now? Eyes on the Road

· · · · · ·

First Things First and Not So Easy

WE ARE AWARE of the hazards with texting and driving, but it's still hard not to do it. It seems so simple: just keep your eyes on the road—or die. Seems like preserving your life would be enough incentive to prevent you from looking at or sending texts. But for some reason, it's not that easy. It's so tempting that we risk our very lives to get that all-important message sent.

The same principle applies at our management meetings. See if this sounds familiar:

You have a 10:00 a.m. management team meeting. So that means you need to get with your team at 9:00 to help you prep for your role at 10:00. That is likely after your 7:30 breakfast meeting. So when you run in for your 10:00 meeting, you're rushed and still processing what you just finished discussing in your previous meeting, and still thinking about next steps from that meeting. You also have a lunch appointment after the management meeting to which you may be late, depending on traffic. So, you're hoping this meeting doesn't run late.

Are you actually present for the 10:00 meeting? You may be physically present but you're mentally distracted and emotionally disconnected. It would seem straightforward—you need to be present in order to be more effective in meetings. But time and time again, we ignore that little order of business of getting present so that we can quickly get to work.

So we give some superficial greeting to one another that is filled with clichés: "How ya doing? . . . Great, how 'bout you? . . . Great! Let's start the meeting!" Then we dive into the agenda.

We attend countless meetings where people are tethered to their electronic devices, reading and sending emails and texts. So, not only are teams not present when they arrive, they continue to distract themselves throughout the meeting.

There is a paradox here that is difficult for our business culture to embrace: we have to go slow to ultimately go faster more effectively.

We talked in the last chapter about how being intentional is showing up and owning your power. The only place you have any power is in this moment, right here, right now. If you are still thinking about this morning's breakfast meeting, you have no power. If you're worried about traffic to get to your lunch appointment, you have no power. If, in this moment, you distract yourself with the electronic buzzes and beeps from electronic devices, you have no power.

The key to being in your power is to be acutely present in this very moment. This takes slowing down at the beginning of the meeting to accept and honor that it takes a few minutes for everyone to get present. This slowing down feels unproductive at the time. But with practice, everyone will realize the benefits of having quality conversations and work that allows you to gain speed as you go through the agenda. Being present will allow for greater clarity in conversations and the ability to move through the agenda more effectively than you would having every-one mentally somewhere else other than where they're sitting.

There is a risk in becoming present. You need to give up immediately attending to the constant stream of "urgencies" that arise from the daily challenges of work and life. The good news is that the risk of becoming present is outweighed by the huge opportunity for growth, power, and fulfillment.

Focus: Check In with MEPS

In all of our offsite work meetings (including phone calls), we invest time upfront to get present. We invite the individuals to start by getting present with themselves and then to open up to becoming present with the others on the team.

Getting present requires intentional focus and at times is unnerving. You can feel uncomfortable in this intentional process because you are used to the safety of being disconnected. Although you may be physically present, you're likely only partially available to the content of the meeting until an issue is raised that matters to you, and you are usually not present enough to connect with the individuals around the table or in the room.

But this is counter to the new way of operating that we have been discussing. If you're going to be more open and vulnerable and show up in your power, then you must shift from disconnection to the intentional practice of connection. This can't be done with lip service. That will actually reinforce that you are NOT in and available for this opportunity to connect. So, it becomes that daily challenge to choose to push yourself out of your comfort zone of disconnection into the vulnerable zone of connection. The good news is that we have plenty of tools to help you get there.

One of our favorite check-in tools that we use with leaders and teams follows the acronym MEPS, which stands for Mentally, Emotionally, Physically, and Spiritually. The question that goes with MEPS is: "Where are you right now?" (not this morning or next week) through four energy centers: the head, the heart, the body, and the soul.

Think of the MEPS process as similar to what happens when you start your car. The car's computer will run through an all-systems check to make sure you are ready to go. Think of this as an all-systems check for yourself.

Where Are You Mentally?—The Head

Where is your mind right now? Sometimes your mind is clear and sharp; sometimes it can be foggy and dull. Sometimes you may be thinking about something so your mind is processing. Sometimes you're mentally multitasking or mentally distracted. Sometimes you feel like you have adult ADD and your mind is all over the place or you've got "monkey mind" as your mind swings from one thought to another. So there are lots of different ways that you may show up mentally. Where are you right now?

Where Are You Emotionally?—The Heart

Yes, this is looking for the "E" word (an emotion). This is the place that is most uncomfortable for us. For a lot of us, we were taught that there is no place in the workplace for emotions. Thankfully, we now know better. Our goal here is not to be a "touchy-feely" group, but to challenge everyone to connect emotionally and empathetically—not only with our heads. Real teams also connect at the heart level with one another. Additionally, we also know that emotional intelligence teaches us that emotions are powerful tools for guidance in our decisions.

There are four basic emotions: mad, sad, glad, scared. The "mad" category includes other emotions such as frustrated, annoyed, irritated, angry, etc. The "sad" category includes hurt, disappointed, grieving, depressed, tender, etc. The "glad" category includes happy, inspired, excited, hopeful, etc. The "scared" category includes anxious, worried, concerned, stressed, etc. Usually we feel multiple emotions at any one point in time. What are you feeling right now?

Where Are You Physically?—The Body

What's going on with your body right now? Maybe you got to the gym so your body is energized with the endorphin high, or you are physically fit. Or maybe you ate pizza last night before going to bed and you're feeling fat or sluggish. Maybe you're fighting off a cold or recovering from the flu. Maybe you're dealing with a headache or backache, or in physical therapy after surgery. Maybe you're sleep deprived so you are tired or exhausted. There are different ways your body can be showing up. What's going on with your body right now?

Where Are You Spiritually?—The Soul

While you can think of this as referring to your soul, you can also consider this as deep beliefs that are core to who you are. Think of this place as where you are in relation to something greater than yourself. This "something" can be nature or a walk along the beach that helps you to connect spiritually. Sometimes it can be family, which can be greater than you. Sometimes it might be a worldview about doing right by people and your community. Sometimes it's embracing the magic of falling in love. Or you might be dazzled by the ever-expanding breakthroughs of science. Sometimes spirituality may be viewed through the lens of religion. And sometimes, it may not apply at this time in your life.

Descriptions of where you are spiritually may include feelings like being grounded or connected, blessed, grateful, searching, disconnected, or not applicable. So where are you right now, in relation to something greater than yourself?

A sample MEPS Check-in that includes all of these categories might sound like this:

Mentally: I'm multitasking. I've got a full plate today with appointments, plus the follow-up from previous ones. I'm also working with my family to figure out what we can do for our vacation this year.

to whoever is checking in so that they can genuinely connect with the speaker, which forces you to shut out the other thoughts in your mind.

Lastly, if someone were to check in, mentally overwhelmed, emotionally distraught, physically spent, and spiritually lost, hopefully the team would stop for a minute and say, "Hey, you sound like you are in a tough place right now. What would support look like for you from the team? Is there anything we can do for you?" We are not robots! We are human beings. At times our lives can get messy. Real teams are there for one another when things get messy—whether it's a personal, family, or business issue.

As you check in with each energy center, even if you're unfocused, emotionally volatile, achy, and dispirited, you are taking a step to being present where you are right now. Once you check in, you are free to take in the presence of the others on the team as they check in with themselves.

Dock It! The Only Place You Have Any Power

Checking in with yourself informs you of the distractions you need to let go of that can prevent you from being present in the moment. You might be thinking or upset about what happened last week. You could be worried about the upcoming month. Both of these situations diminish your power right now. The only place you have any power is in *this* moment.

We've been using a device we call Dock It! It's a simple exercise that you can access anywhere, anytime, to identify and separate all of the things on your to-do list that are swirling through your mind and taking you away from being in the moment.

You may be worried about making the end-of-month or final-quarter numbers. Or there may be something more personal, perhaps related to your family. It's normal to have these kinds of thoughts and distractions, a kind of swirl of responsibilities and logistics as you go about your day.

Typically, we act like we aren't distracted in the moment. We try to stuff or repress the noise that clouds our mind or emotions. But that generally backfires, because the more we try to act like something's not bothering us, telling ourselves to just NOT think about it for now, the more we actually DO think about it.

So rather than acting like it's not there and distracting you, the best way to let some of the energy dissipate from the distraction is to actually speak about what it is that is distracting you and let it go—Dock It!

Imagine for a moment that outside of your offices there is a lake, and from the shore going into the lake is a dock. The metaphorical dock is a safe place to temporarily and safely store those distractions.

A simple question for everyone on the team to answer is, "What's currently preventing you from being fully present right now—what could you put on the dock for now, knowing that after the meeting you can pick it back up and take it with you?"

A response to this type of question might be: " I have a lunch meeting that I'm concerned about today. I know that my timing is tight for traffic. So I need to dock that for now."

This allows everyone to speak to what those items are and dock them until after the meeting. Speaking to these items invites everyone to connect with you and where you are and allows you to actually dock these items and minimize how distracting they may be for you. By acknowledging that distractions exist and intentionally declaring them to be on the dock, you help yourself refrain from thinking about them.

While you can go through this preparatory exercise on your own at any time, we've found it productive in a team setting. After we check in, we invite anyone to speak about what he or she needs to dock.

Once you are aware of the list, choose to set aside or dock the distractions until you are ready to access them in the appropriate moment. You are being clear with yourself as to your intention (being present) and taking action as to what could consciously (or even unconsciously) inhibit you from focusing on what's in front of you (identifying and separating out the clutter). Now you can invite all of the power you have inside to emerge.

We were engaged by a fast-growth tech services company to help them develop a rhythm for their management meeting structure. They found that most of their planned meetings were canceled or indefinitely postponed because of the fast-paced and unpredictable nature of client demands and other intervening events. So they devoted little time to team collaboration and often made key decisions by text and email. They wanted our guidance to help them break that cycle.

In our discovery work with the team, we learned that the team members thought meetings were a waste of time. It wasn't even true that they were canceled because of other priorities, just that they dreaded the meeting; it was easy to come up with why they should postpone it. So we probed into why the meetings were so unproductive. They uniformly advised us that it seemed that meetings interrupted the rhythm of the workday and that it was challenging to drop the rapid flow of activity and attend them. To compensate, they would show up at the meeting, either in person or via conference when on the road, and multitask to keep the momentum of whatever they were working on. It was clear to us that the team set themselves up to fail at the meetings by continuing to focus on other urgent distractions.

Not surprisingly, we were given a three-hour time slot to meet with the team (quite short for our practice, yet a feat of endurance from their experience). Our sole intention was to show them how to get present. We started with a check-in, first a tutorial, and then we modeled it authentically in real time. When it was their turn, the process invited a cascade of mental fatigue and streams of consciousness with twists, turns, and gyrations. No wonder they were distracted!

Finally, we taught them to dock those distractions. Not forever. Just for three hours. We even made it physical by creating a partitioned space (the dock) in the meeting room and offered them to write the distractions (each and every element of the mental fatigue) and place them safely and temporarily on the dock. One by one, they agreed to Dock It! Progressively we—and they—felt new energy emerging.

It is here that each team member was connecting to themselves and getting in their power. In this place of discomfort, members brought more of themselves and became open to receive more from the others on the team.

It may be uncomfortable, though when you lean into that discomfort, you can grow. In the growth that comes afterward we build trust.

Stepping into Your Voice: Truth and Trust

When you slow your meeting down in order to check in, dock distractions, and really get present, you have also done something that is crucial for you and the team to actually show up: you've created safety. If people are distracted or banging out emails while someone else is talking, the message is that what you're saying isn't that important. In other words, it's not safe for you to be more transparent and vulnerable.

There is no way that people will really show up with their deepest perspectives and thoughts when it's not safe. But getting present is the first critical step toward creating the safety that will help people be more open.

You have now created the opportunity to speak your truth and co-create a container of trust. This is the time to show up with what is coming up for you. Now is the time to share exactly what is on your mind from your beautifully unique perspectives, experiences, filters, history, and education. This is the time and place for your voice!

If you're feeling uncomfortable, the discomfort is a signal to you that you are taking a risk. This risk can and ultimately will create a closer bond of trust when you meet the others on the team in the middle of that discomfort, and then together, you discover more about each other and create a new, shared truth. Afterward, you are more comfortable with each other and trust each other more. You have made the shift from discomfort to comfort, from mistrust to trust.

And, more importantly, you can do it again, as there is always an opportunity to find a new discomfort and grow. Your presence gives the team permission to take the next step by each speaking your truth, even if it is difficult, hard to speak, and uncomfortable to hear. You are building trust.

The more you go through the process of truth sharing, the deeper your level of trust becomes. And, when you feel that trust, you are each more likely to reach for and stretch into the next level of challenge, because you have learned that it is actually easier and more beneficial to do it together rather than by yourself.

One of the ways that you can continue to build trust with your teammates is by validating their ideas and thoughts. You wouldn't need to do this all the time, but when you hear someone take a risk, perhaps by challenging current thinking or voicing a dissenting opinion, you can validate them and their ideas by mirroring back to them the essence of what you heard. This validation helps to affirm for them that you understood them and that their opinion is welcome, even if it's different from yours.

Here's an example of validating someone's ideas or opinions. When we worked with the broader leadership team of a retail chain, approximately twenty people, the discussion was focused on what people really liked about the "store experience." One of the leaders stood up and said, "At the risk of upsetting everyone, I respectfully have to disagree. Each of our stores has a slightly different look and feel. How the merchandise is set up has become solely store managers' discretion. Even the music that is played is different from store to store. While I do agree that store managers should be able to tailor their merchandise to their particular demographics and customer wants, I think the overall look and feel of the experience needs to be much more consistent."

The president immediately got up and said, "Thank you so much for saying that. I said at the beginning of this meeting that I really want us to be open and honest and transparent with our thoughts and ideas because I believe it will help us to make better decisions. So I hear your impression that our store experience has gotten so dissimilar as to dilute what our brand is all about."

The president was validating this person's comments. This person had taken a risk to show up with his truth about the store experience. After the president had validated this risk taking, everyone else started taking risks and the conversation got to the heart of where their challenges were.

Even for the high-tech team that hated meetings (from our earlier example), we knew that our initial three-hour meeting would only get us so far, even though we were confident that the first experience in getting present would pay its dividends. We were right. The second meeting was scheduled for five hours. We checked in, docked our distractions, and their collective presence prepared them to enter into the trust minefield.

They opened up by sharing the bad and ugly stuff that they had ignored or stored up. Their presence helped them actively listen. They were openly curious, not defensive. They were vulnerable. From this place of presence, they were able to keep their attention on the most important business challenge of the group and ultimately collaborate as a team.

The Promised Land: Connecting with Presence

The most important thing in our meetings is not to cover every last bullet point, but to feel like we have deeply connected as a team, that we strengthened the safety of the group, and felt our trust growing. We will eventually get through the important content of the agenda, but the priority is to actually feel the deepening sense of fulfillment that comes from being in your power, giving all that you have to give, and looking around the table and feeling that everyone else is too.

This is when the magic happens. Trust grows, and people feel safe to bring their opinions and ideas without being judged for them. You will actually cover more ground because, at this point, INpowerment has taken over. The synergy of the group is in action. Although you may have intentionally started the meeting out slowly, now the group is connecting and processing at a whole new level of clarity, engagement, and speed.

Being present for all of your energy centers provides the foundation for stepping into and connecting with your power. There is a paradox at play—the more we take the risk to show our true selves, the more we fear we (our opinions and ideas) will be rejected. Although we may think this will push us away from those we need to work with, we actually grow CLOSER to those folks. There is a deeper understanding of one another. There is TRUST! This trust becomes a beautiful fuel for the next engagement to continue the momentum.

As you all become present in the moment, you will sense a different energy in the room. It is palpable. The same bodies are around the table, but the communal spirit is heightened. Each of you is bringing more of yourselves by connecting with your presence.

Invited back by our high-tech team for a third round, they allocated an entire day for us. They had bought in and were willing to invest—not just in us, but also in themselves!

The team now had proof that becoming present together in the moment is the critical predicate to developing a productive rhythm for meeting structure. Now it was easy for us as a group to co-create a meeting platform to generate value. This time around, we asked the team to lead their check-in. Without prompting they instinctively and safely docked their many distractions, and set themselves up for connecting with presence. We facilitated a heated yet moving exploration around big wants, deep fears, and perceived blocks that opened the team to surprising revelations and earned trust. One member shared that she was afraid of showing her anxiety because all her life she was competing to be seen as a strong person rather than the image she had of herself as a scared little girl. A young senior executive explained that he thought he was supposed to have all of the answers because of his status, so instead of letting others know when he's puzzled, he either shouts over everyone to quiet down his own insecurity or stays quiet to mask his lack of confidence. In this admission, he earned trust by more fully revealing and explaining the motivations behind his behavior, which others had assumed was simply arrogance. Now he was out, owned it for himself, and finally stepped into his power through his honest and complete presence.

The post-meeting feedback was consistent: they had never realized that when everyone focused on one thing—what's most important to the team—they all become faster and wiser. That's the theme for the rhythm to which they now all subscribe.

Short Version of MEPS

The first step is to check in with your energy centers. Where are you right now:

- Mentally (in your head)—are you clear or distracted? Focused or in a stream of consciousness?

- Emotionally (in your heart)—what is the range of your feelings: glad, mad, sad, scared, ashamed, guilty, or tender? Are you feeling more than one?

- Physically (in your body)—as you scan your body right now, do you feel achy, tight, fit, hungry, or tired?

- Spiritually (in your soul)—are you connecting (or not) to

something bigger than yourself? That could be nature, purpose or calling, higher power, connection to people, or perhaps right now there is lack of connection.

CHAPTER 14

Rules of Engagement

· · · · · ·

Need for Norms: Tell Me How to Play the Game

IN THE LAST chapter we discussed how getting present is crucial to INpowering yourself and your teammates. Assuming everyone is present, connected, and engaged—now what? Even if you are starting to buy into our premise that vulnerability and transparency are critical, there is still a need to understand HOW to actually show up in a safe way.

When you are traveling on the roadways, there are laws, signs, and proper etiquette that promote driving safely and effectively. We all understand the laws and guidelines, and, for the most part, we honor and embrace them (otherwise there would be total chaos on roadways). Through those guidelines, we form a social contract for safety.

Our common experience is that people in relationships gravitate to safe ways of engaging with others. The same is true for our teams. We need to create a sense of safety and provide a safe way to openly express ourselves.

A cultural communication revolution requires the establishment of guidelines that everyone can embrace and honor. These guidelines lay out specifically how we are going to connect with one another to honor confidential conversations, encourage open and honest dialogue, commit to speaking individual truths, and include emotional context for where the team is so they know how to process our interactions.

Guidelines for Team Interaction

We use our set of guidelines for working with groups of various sizes, from one person to small and large groups. They're flexible. The guidelines are both simple and aspirational. Initially, we used them to help us facilitate. Over time, we've learned that they actually help everyone step into their power.

We'll show you how to use these guidelines and protocol as the framework to be safe, go deep, and make cultural shift achievable. We've provided you first with the list of guidelines and their definitions, followed by a deeper explanation.

1. I will respect confidentiality

Whatever happens in a conversation or meeting stays with the participants, unless the owner(s) of what was shared explicitly consent to sharing. Every team needs to be able to invoke confidentiality when necessary. Sensitive issues can arise, whether they are personal, family or business related, tactical or strategic, financial, or involve human resources, and the team needs to be able to have an open and frank discussion without worrying about whether information will be leaked to other coworkers. This guideline provides an invitation for team members to dig deeper in their truth arsenal.

2. I will be present in the moment

Right here, right now, participants commit to showing up with their full presence. Last chapter we discussed doing MEPS and Dock It! check-ins to help get present. Only you know how distracted you are—or can easily become. You have to make it a point to stay present and engaged.

3. I will stay when times get tough

If the conversation goes to a vulnerable or difficult place, participants must agree not only to remain physically present, but also mentally and emotionally. This is when teams have to pull together to support one another through difficult times. This is how we know that we have each other's backs. This also applies to the times that there are struggles within the team or differences of opinion that can feel tough to find solutions for. As a team you need to be strong enough to hold the discomfort and allow for discovery.

4. I will speak my truth

Participants must take ownership for sharing stories from their essence—truths unique to them. This is the basis of INpowerment. This is actually all you have to offer your team. This is a commitment to bring your voice and show up. Notice that there's a lower case "t" on this truth. You are not speaking a universal TRUTH. This is just your truth.

5. I will ask for what I want

Participants pledge to come from a sovereign place and ask for their big want (without expectation of always getting it exactly). You are responsible to make sure you have everything you need to be successful in your role. You are responsible to ask for those things that are important to you. Nobody is a mind reader. So it's crucial that you and everyone else on the team are INpowered to ask for what you want. You may not get what you want, but you won't know for certain if you don't ask.

6. I will take care of myself

Participants own their responsibility to mind their energy and adjust to their teammates accordingly. You are responsible for you. If something isn't working for you, then you need to speak up and address it. If you need help or need to discuss a difficult issue with the group, it's up to you to ask for time and get it on the agenda. This guideline complements number 5 above.

7. I will express and own my feelings

Share your emotions in context and take responsibility for your feelings as belonging to you, without expecting that others will feel the same. This is an intentional commitment to learn how to be more emotionally intelligent. Identifying what you are feeling in the moment and expressing that emotion is your commitment to your team in an ongoing effort to create more connective authentic relationships.

8. I will own my perspectives

Your perspectives are your beliefs and opinions. They're shaped by the way you view the world. Our perspectives reflect our experience during the conversation. You are INpowered to speak, using your perspective and experience, when you own it as yours by simply adding, "it's my perspective," "it is my opinion," etc. Owning your perspective is part of speaking your truth. That being said, it doesn't mean your perspective is always right or true. It just means it's true for you.

9. I will actively listen

Bring all your senses to interactions and use them to receive data and emotion using your head and heart. Hear the silence between words. Observe gestures. Process and embrace all the energy. Active listening speaks to being engaged in the act of listening. This is not a passive, normal form of listening. Active listening actually requires that you first turn off the way you might normally listen. For most of us, we absorb information by thinking in terms of problem solving. You should suspend this "listen to fix" mode initially, because that will take you into the process of developing ideas to help this person. When this happens, you are no longer listening or engaged with the person.

You also want to turn off the part of you that may be forming a perspective or assessing what this person is saying and wondering why they did this or that. Assessing the person will also take you out of listening to them. After suspending those natural instincts, you will empathically engage with this person. What is their body language? What are they feeling? Why is this topic so important to them? Put yourself in their shoes and try to truly connect with them, taking in the information they are sharing as if you were going to have to repeat it back to them. This is what active listening is all about.

10. I will speak respectfully, without blaming, shaming, or fixing

Team members show respect for each other when they claim responsibility for their parts, rather than blaming others. When an entire team lifts blame from the group, they create an environment where each member seeks to improve themselves rather than fix others. Blame is defined as a way to discharge pain and suffering. You want to have an open debate about issues and opportunities before the team, but you always need to be respectful of one another. There is no place for rude or abusive tones or language. So if you find yourself wanting to blame somebody, it is to make yourself feel better.

11. I will ask permission before offering feedback or advice

Those of you that are professional fixers, remember that any unsolicited advice will be received as criticism! So if you find yourself saying, "What you need to do is . . . " or "Have you thought about trying . . . ?" you've fallen into the advice-giving trap.

By asking someone before you give them feedback, you increase the feeling of safety and the person to whom you're speaking is more likely to receive your offer. This is the way to safely offer advice—ask permission. Just simply say, "I have an idea for you, are you open to discussing it?" Or, "I have some experience with that type of situation that I'd be happy to share. Is now a good time?" It's the simple pause before speaking that makes it safe for you to share what's on your mind. If the person says yes—go for it!

12. I am willing to make mistakes

Learn to fail or fail to learn is a framework for a growth (rather than fixed) mindset. To be INpowered is to embrace failure. And, because we aren't a computer or a robot, mistakes come with being human!

13. I am willing to laugh at myself

We can't take ourselves too seriously. Our work is serious. Business is serious. But, don't be wound so tight that you can't have a good laugh along the way. The best team we know laughs a lot! Safety has allowed them to drop their defenses, which not only allows team members to speak more openly about sensitive issues, it allows them to embrace spontaneity and playfulness, joy and lightheartedness. So, enjoy the journey with your colleagues.

14. I will be on time and stay until the end

Show respect for the others by all agreeing on a schedule for a meeting and then sticking to it. Be punctual! Everyone is super busy. Everyone's time is valuable. Respect one another and respect yourself. Honor your commitment to the team with punctual starts as well as punctual stops!

15. I will turn off all electronics

Use your device as a tool to stay present rather than an instrument to distract you from being in the meeting. Electronics are an epidemic for individuals and teams. Turn off all electronics or put them into airplane mode. Many teams we work with have a basket for phones so everyone can drop them in at the beginning of the meeting and pick them up on the way out. Do it! You will survive! People will figure things out without you. It's like being on a flight that doesn't have Wi-Fi—you can't connect, and you get over it because you don't have the choice. Here we invite you to choose connection with your teammates.

These fifteen guidelines are designed for one thing: encouraging a sense of safety! So honor and embrace them both individually and collectively to create the safest environment for you and your team to express yourselves.

Permission to Speak Freely: Framework, Not Rules

Notice that we spoke about the previous norms as guidelines, not rules. You've grown up with lots of rules, especially involving teams and competition. Do this; don't do that. You learned the boundaries and tried your best to play within them while looking for ways to circumvent when possible and as needed to win. Often, dodging rules is even part of playing the game. It is said that rules are meant to be broken. So we've jettisoned the "rules" and instead introduced "guidelines." We believe that guidelines are flexible enough to grow with changing and unexpected circumstances. We encourage teams to use these guidelines as a starting point, and then tailor them to their own group as they go along.

As an example, you can be flexible with the guideline "I will turn off all electronics." There may be occasions when a pending urgent call trumps total presence in a meeting.

Many times the team will add new guidelines that become important for the team to be intentional about. Maybe these new guidelines are based on the company's core values or purpose. Sometimes there are guidelines that don't seem to fit and are deleted.

Remember that guidelines support conversation. They are not there to have structure for structure's sake. They are there to help the discussion be more deep and open. It's okay to go off script at times and it's okay if conversations are a bit messy! You can handle messy. Just know that you can go back to the guidelines to help clean up.

The intention of these guidelines is to create a safe environment by providing structure with implicit permission for team members to own those boundaries and speak their truth about what works for them. We once worked with a pharmaceutical consulting firm and they customized their own placard of guidelines after working with ours for a few meetings. When we came back the next quarter and brought out our guidelines, they were initially embarrassed to insert their version. We told them we were delighted they took ownership of the idea and that this affirmed the true spirit of their flexibility for us.

This Is a Game Changer: Aspirational

As you read through the guidelines, they seem simple. That's because they are easy to understand and process. They probably seem straightforward, but did you notice yourself saying, "I can't do that" or "Really?" or "How am I going to do that?" or "That's a stretch for me!"

That's because these guidelines are aspirational! Being aspirational means appreciating that each of the guidelines is along a spectrum: on one end is the simple, face-value interpretation and on the other end is the complex, deeper opportunity. For example, "I will speak my truth" has multiple levels. You can simply speak your truth on the surface, and yet there are infinite levels of depth to which you can open and share more of your truth. Nobody shows up being able to actually enact these guidelines or follow them perfectly. Ever! We've been using these for over twenty years and still make mistakes. Thankfully, making mistakes is covered!

For most leaders, there will be guidelines that you are more experienced or comfortable executing. But there will also be those that will push you out of your comfort zone. Take owning your emotions, for example. For most of you that is a stretch. Another guideline that is tough is to always be actively listening. It is so hard to shut off our normal tendencies to problem solve, assess, or debate, that to actually be fully listening is a struggle. And, almost everyone begins twitching when you first collect their cell phones. You know which guidelines are going to be more challenging than others. Accept the challenge. This is a great opportunity to grow.

We believe the guidelines are life changing. We introduce them at management team retreats as well as regular meetings. We also have seen them work when integrated in life at home or with the community. They become a roadmap for how to behave with others, both on and off the playing field.

Commitment to the Guidelines

We encourage you to embrace these guidelines as if they were an agreement between you and your team to show up and honor those guidelines every day. Buying in and agreeing to the guidelines means you are making a commitment to a new way of engagement and it is critical. Although we believe these guidelines can easily be one-size-fits-all, you can modify them as your team requires. This is a way of engaging with your team. Do it daily!

Commit to the guidelines as specific, yet aspirational. They are not vague platitudes! Quote them, as part of your daily language, in corporate rituals, meetings, and interactions. Our teams enjoy saying: "I'm taking care of myself," or "I'm asking for what I want," when they interrupt to make a broader point or gracefully exit the room for an emergency. In a quarterly board meeting of one of our clients who has ritualized the guidelines, we witnessed the team embody "I will actively listen" when a board member gave unsolicited feedback that she truly appreciated being heard and seen by her peers.

Each of you will be on a path to growth. These guidelines become an opportunity to hold each other accountable to your agreement. They will effectively change your organization's culture. Once your management team embraces these guidelines, others will want to take them back to their departments. Over time, the entire organization will be running with these principles.

The team has to make the commitment to the guidelines. It is not easy, but it will open the gateway to future conversations that will elevate the performance of your team. It will also elevate your own performance and overall fulfillment as your voice—your power—is ever present.

The beautiful thing about these guidelines is that they are transferable to other domains of our lives, not just work. Once we were working with the CEO of a young tech start-up. They were growing by leaps and bounds. When he and his team embraced these guidelines, his response was, "Oh my God, these aren't just for the board room or management team, these are guidelines to live my life by!"

This is a very common response. Once people begin to figure out how to create safety and be more open and transparent at work, why wouldn't they want to be that way with the people they care most about in the world—their spouses, kids, family, and friends? They do! And you can too! Leverage your experience at work to practice and learn how to use the guidelines, and then take them into your other domains.

These guidelines are a framework to keep things safe so you can work. They are a path to the safety of mutual respect and honor the breadth and depth of truth with compassion for others and ourselves. They help you engage at a deeper level and embrace the creative tension that comes from diversity, exploration, and shared discovery.

CHAPTER 15

Wow, Honesty! Navigating Rocky Roads

• • • • • •

Clear It

WHILE CLEAR GUIDELINES provide a roadmap for how we conduct ourselves as we interact, we need a specific tool to safely harness the rich content that will provide lively debate and enliven the subtle differences among the team, with the diverse opinions contributing to the team's winning differentiators. It's vital to be able to keep conflict from getting out of control and to keep debate healthy so you can create strong buy-in and commitment from your team.

As the team comes together, we ask: What is getting in the way of you showing up with your voice and power? Is there something that is holding you back from being here, right now, with everything you've got? When a team member is holding back a concern or issue with another team member or with the team, that issue needs to be cleared.

How do you know when you have an issue that needs to be cleared? You will likely be emotionally stirred up as you attempt to reconnect with the individuals on your team. You may notice that your internal dialogue wants you to shut down or withhold how much you share. Sometimes you may feel an emotional trigger someplace in your body— perhaps your belly, neck, head, or shoulders. Triggers are blocks to the openness you are looking for. It's a physical message that you're not yet ready to fully engage until you clear it out. Each of your emotional triggers will prevent you from being able to have an authentic connection with the person or group that you are feeling triggered by.

Think about the reactions you've gotten at home with your significant other. If he or she has been triggered by you and is in a deep emotional reaction (mad, sad, scared), is it possible to get into a constructive conversation about how to resolve or fix problems and move forward? No.

The same holds true for you and your business colleagues. Our tendency is to jump right in to the content of the agenda. But, if people are holding these triggers with one another, the resulting conversation will be superficial.

The only way to create the trust necessary to get back into a deeper conversation is to clear the trigger. We anticipate meetings will require two steps:

1. *Clearing any triggers*

2. *Stepping into content*

When you think about the triggers, think about them as your experience of someone else's behavior, either verbal or non-verbal. When you experience these behaviors, you will have a reaction based on your unique background, education, work, and relational experience. Sometimes the reactions are positive, and sometimes they are negative. It doesn't make your reactions right or wrong, or the other person's behavior right or wrong—it's simply true that you've been triggered.

If your reactions are strong enough to prevent you from fully stepping into the content on the agenda, then you need to clear how you've been triggered.

This clearing out of the issue will create a powerful dialogue that may be scary at first, but will later be rewarding for you and the team. The natural fear is that the clearing would somehow hurt relationships and create more of a divide between you and the other person or group, when, paradoxically, just the opposite happens. You actually become closer. Trust is strengthened and the entire team is taken to a deeper level.

The reason this is true goes back to the process that groups (two or more people) go through in their development of authentic community: pseudo-community, chaos, and discovery.

An authentic community is where we are more open, transparent, and genuinely showing up as who we are. It is where we bring our power, our voice, to the group as the gift it is meant to be. When we are in authentic community, we are ready for the content of the agenda, and can thrive as a true team because we bring synergy to be harnessed.

The key to getting into authentic community is to go through chaos. You can't go around it or superficially get to authenticity. You have to go directly into the chaos to get to the community to which you aspire.

Think of it this way. Do you typically learn more or grow more during times of smooth sailing of during times of adversity? Classically, we learn through our challenges, mistakes, failures, or crises.

So our recommendation is to "embrace the chaos." This means that you as a group are committed to stepping into difficult conversations, sharing your perceptions and experiences, and clearing the triggers that prevent you from being in authentic relationships with colleagues. We had one management team that framed this process as "clearing the crap," because that's what it felt like had been building up—a bunch of crap that was preventing the team from getting to the heart of real issues.

Five-Step Clearing Process

The actual clearing process is reasonably straightforward, but it's a process nonetheless. As such, it will take some getting used to by the team before it feels easy to use. This process can be a bit clumsy at first and not very conversational, because you are guided to put your thoughts into five distinct buckets. But it doesn't take long for the clumsiness to give way to a more natural clearing conversation.

When you get a hit on an issue, we suggest a five-step process to identify and separate the clutter:

1. What are the facts?

A small part of your issue is grounded in facts, so it helps to parse those bits of provable, objective data first. Facts reflect actions or omissions, statements made, and potentially your reactions to the data. Examples of factual statements include:

You committed to have the manager reviews completed by Friday and they are not yet done.

You have worked late every night this week preparing for this morning's client meeting.

This team has been working together for less than one year.

I'm currently separating from my husband.

These are all factual statements that you can support, and they lay the foundation for the perspectives and feelings that follow.

2. What are your perspectives?

These are your opinions and beliefs that come from your point of view. Your point of view may not match that of the person with whom you're clearing, but it's still your truth—with a small "t." In the clearing process, as with the guidelines, you own your perspectives. This keeps the person or team you're clearing with safe from any projections.

3. What are you feeling?

Do you remember any physical sensation you have experienced about the issue? That physical feeling was associated with an emotion. You may have multiple feelings triggered, or one may be pronounced. By identifying and speaking about the identified emotion, you are liberating or clearing yourself from them.

4. What was your role in attracting the issue to you?

Stuff doesn't just happen to people. Rather, they have a role or responsibility in why they attracted whatever situation they were a part of. In this critical step, you share what your part may have been in creating the issue. By exploring and describing this, you invite the person you're clearing with to better see and understand why you may be sensitive to their behavior and what it is about you that elicits your reaction or response. It also allows you to claim responsibility for your part of the issue, making it easier—and safer—for the other party to also claim what may be his or her part.

5. What do you want specifically?

Now you have the opportunity to ask for what you want. You may not necessarily get it. Though if you don't ask, you'll never know. This request is also the platform for what resolution may follow the discussion. The more specific and clear you are about what you want, the more likely you will get what you really need.

Mirror to Show Understanding

After you have gone through the five steps, one of the people involved in the issue or someone from the group should mirror back what they heard the other person say. They should mirror it using the same five steps, and use as many of the person's original words as they can. The idea behind this is that it shows whoever has been trying to clear an issue that they have truly been heard and seen.

When you are mirroring what another person has said, it is not the time to debate what was expressed, explain your side of the situation, or make any interpretations of what was said. You simply, but genuinely, repeat back what you heard.

Mirroring is also not meant to be a test. So if you forget something that the other person said, like their emotion or want, just ask the other person to please restate it. The key is that the person with the trigger ultimately feels like they have been heard.

We were recently having dinner with the CEO, CFO, and COO of a large distribution company. During the evening, a beautiful example of the clearing process showed up organically. The COO said to the CEO:

"The facts are that you responded to several emails from my managers, who had copied you as an FYI. They spoke to me about how it seems as though you don't trust them.

"My perspective is that you have a hard time not getting caught up in the details of the business and can't help being a micromanager. I also believe that when you do that, it undermines my authority and me.

"Additionally, my opinion is that you rarely, if ever, speak of anything positive that I or anyone else on the team has accomplished.

"These things make me feel frustrated, angry, and concerned.

"For my part, I haven't done a good job at helping you to pull out of the details of the business. I work hard to do a good job, so I'm sensitive when people seem to not trust me.

"I want to work with you to make sure you feel close to what's going on in the business without having you micromanage the operations.

"I also want you to recognize that we have grown 10 to 20 percent over the past five years, so the team is doing a lot of things right. I'd like you to begin recognizing their positive contributions."

After the COO finished speaking, the CEO did a beautiful job of mirroring. He responded:

"Thanks for expressing all of that; let me make sure that I heard you. The facts are that I responded to several emails, and members of your team actually came up and spoke to you about my responses and that they expressed concern that I didn't trust them.

"Your perspective is I can't help but to dive into details because I'm a micromanager—which I am and totally own, by the way.

"You also feel that it undermines you, and you also observe that I only focus on the negatives and rarely point out any positive accomplishments.

"This frustrates you and makes you angry and concerned.

"Your role in this situation is that you haven't done a very good job of helping me to pull out of the details. You are also sensitive to people when they don't trust you, because you work very hard to be on top of everything.

"What you want is for us to work together to find the right level of engagement that keeps me plugged in but doesn't undermine your authority. You also want me to honor and acknowledge the accomplishments that come with amazing growth over the last five years.

"Did I get that right?"

The COO felt heard by the CEO, and the trigger was effectively cleared. They ultimately left dinner feeling a deep sense of connection and alignment.

One key predicate for the success of the clearing process is to know that it isn't about changing the other person or group. It is literally about clearing your emotional charge that would otherwise prevent you from authentic connection. If you go into the clearing process expecting change, you've lost! A resolution may be needed to address the circumstances of your clearing, but that comes later.

Return to INtegrity

What makes the clearing process work is an understanding that no one is trying to hurt or embarrass anyone personally. Everyone has a common objective—to be the best that they can be, individually and collectively. We bring our healthy debate to the fore with that common intention. The result is that you are aligned with yourself, the other individuals, and the group.

When you are clearing triggers, you need to leave your ego (and even at times your title) at the door. Clearing is about sharing our perceptions about one another and growing as leaders and as a team. You need to be able to not take things personally, which is easier said than done. If you find yourself triggered by someone clearing with you, many times you will need to just sit with your reaction and breathe for a bit. You will find that your trigger was simply your feelings getting hurt or the result of having taken the clearing personally. When you realize this is the case, you are able to let go of your own trigger.

If not, maybe you have a different perspective that you need to now clear. This would mean that you are now triggered in a way that would prevent you from being fully present for the core of today's agenda. That's a legitimate clearing for you. Go ahead and initiate a clearing from your perspective. Note that the "facts" may be the same.

Your objective is to feel confident that you can bring ALL of your perspectives to the group and be accepted, rather than judged. Clearing these triggers is the way for you to gain confidence and trust in the group. This will show you that the team can accept your difference of opinion or perspectives and honor your truth.

At the end of the day, the most successful teams openly challenge one another's ideas and thoughts. This robust exchange leads to not only the best decisions for the company, but also the deepest fulfillment for its leaders. Colleagues get to bring their experience and diversity

CHAPTER 17

Making Our Way: Use It or Lose It

• • • • • •

Now, That's What I'm Talking About— Creating a Rhythm

WHEN TEAM MEMBERS return to the office after an offsite, they often exclaim, "Wow! That retreat was awesome." Sharing our life-changing experiences, connecting to people and to a greater goal, and coming together with genuine and selfless connection make it inspiring. To sustain the momentum from a single positive experience of this new culture at the retreat, you must create rituals that can be practiced as part of a new rhythm that the team embraces.

We've had some awesome three-day experiences and tried catching up with the team months later, only to find out that they were back to their old ways with no sustainable change. One in particular comes to mind. We coached a law firm partners' retreat for three days with outstanding reviews. The retreat aimed to address lack of engagement at their meetings, divisiveness, siloed departments, and an inability to master conflict in a healthy and productive way. We shared the tools from the previous chapters. The lawyers understood the value of these new approaches while we were together and made some progress with healthy confrontation, sharing perspectives, and identifying opportunities for resolution.

After the retreat, we recommended the partners continue to utilize the tools and we suggested that we facilitate one of the next meetings. They turned us down. Though we tried connecting a few times, it was almost a year before we received a call from the managing partner asking us to help with an intervention between two partners. He admitted that they went back to work after the retreat and barely gave lip service to the tools. The partner took responsibility for not insisting on creating a rhythm that would stick.

There are no silver bullets for creating change within an organization. Change comes because everyone buys into the desired outcome. From there, it takes intentional focus to ensure that change happens.

For groups to connect at a deeper level, the key is to establish a rhythm for your new connection. You can do things like schedule a weekly meeting of the leadership team, a monthly conference call with regional counterparts to discuss challenges and opportunities, or quarterly reviews of budget compared to plan. These recurring connections create a rhythm of genuine engagement opportunities with your workmates and harness the depth of perspective and insight from everyone in the organization.

Authentic connection is the cornerstone to support this underutilized asset.

Short Shelf Life: Reset the Default

We've all enjoyed a mountaintop experience, only to return to work and have that energy sucked up by the force of the status quo and daily life.

The momentum of the experience can be lost within a few days or weeks. Unless the new connection is integrated into the normal cadence of how a group engages, the shelf life of that genuine connection will be fleeting. Everyone will revert back to their comfort zone or to how they first learned to react when they are stressed, so leaders need to reset default procedures to be consistent with the new rhythm.

A default is the baseline to which we return in times of chaos, stress, or tension, whenever we don't have the capacity to take a step back, get present, and take notice of what is happening. So, to remedy the conundrum, change the baseline. This change takes time and practice, though it can be accomplished with sustainable success in less than a month—but it still takes work. A mountaintop experience sets us up for success and helps accelerate the time for reset, but we still need at least three weeks of vigilant practice.

There needs to be a sense of urgency around adhering to the new rhythm. If two meetings go by without staff using the new protocols, the new procedures will be shelved. That's all it takes, two meetings. It's scary how quickly you lose what you worked so hard to create.

So, we urge our clients to immediately anchor the authenticity takeaways by using the same tools we introduced while they were at the retreat, including checking in to get present (using MEPS and Dock It!), committing to guidelines (to reinforce their aspirational quality), and creating space early on the agenda for clearing elephants in the room. Yes—clearing should take place at every meeting, no exception. It creates safety to embrace the complexity of the agenda's content.

Moreover, team members will relate the rhythm of the tools introduced during the mountaintop experience, which serves to reinforce the positivity of the new way of being. After a few weeks of regular practice, the natural rhythm of the tools will organically change the old baseline and you have successfully reset your organization's default.

Make This Process YOUR Own

Who owns the new normal? Who's responsible for making sure that this process is followed? YOU. You and every other team member take ownership and responsibility individually and collectively.

You and the team have worked too hard creating this new, connected experience and energy to simply let it slip away. We can provide you with the key elements to anchor and integrate this experience so that you can sustain your momentum, and set it up for growth. But, ultimately you need to take responsibility to ensure everyone shows up and honors the commitment to change.

Once groups have experienced how much deeper they can be with one another and how richly connected dialogue and fulfillment can be, they may not realize these results take commitment, work, and time. It's tempting to go back to the comfort of complacency and superficial connections. So, it's up to everyone to make sure this change is integrated into your new lives.

Make These Tools Your Own

The tools we've suggested may work for your team in its current form, or you may need to make some adjustments; either way; it's important for you to embrace the tools as your own.

Here are some suggestions:

1. Use the tools that worked best for you at the retreat or offsite. If, for example, Dock It! was powerful when you experienced it at the offsite, start with it before you check in with MEPS.

2. Modify tools so they are unique to you and your team. For example, one of our clients named the clearing tool "Clear the Crap" and another used "Elephant Herding"—terms that were used during

the offsite. Another client added a few guidelines that were specific to their team.

3. Transition from characterizing the tools as "the Shift 180 tools" to "Our Tools"—they belong to you.

4. Make placards of your customized list of guidelines, MEPS, and the clearing process for every team member to keep in an accessible place. At the start of the process, use these cheat sheets to help reinforce what they've just learned.

When we returned to the law firm for a second try, we shifted our approach by giving them planning homework to create their own version of tools and meeting structure, and then let them lead the connection process. We knew they had talent preparing for complex litigation and corporate planning, so why not have them leverage those gifts and apply them inward? We helped them create a safe environment and then provided the guidelines to keep them on course. After a day and a half, the group of managing partners co-created a system that had their mark on it, and ultimately they were able to get buy-in from the partners. Because now the changes were proprietary—they owned them.

Anchor and Integrate

To assure that change stays with your organization instead of becoming a fleeting flirtation, you need to anchor and integrate new processes and systems. Here are some specific actions that you can take to anchor and integrate this experience:

Use Processes More Rather than Less

There are many times during the day that doing a MEPS at your desk can help you get present before a call or other work you're trying to accomplish. You can also do MEPS before you get home, so you are more present with your family. Use the tools more, especially at first, to get accustomed to how they work.

Integrate Processes in Every Meeting and Interaction for Three Weeks

Yes, in every interaction. If you drop in on a colleague for an impromptu meeting, check in first. When your colleague asks you, "How are you doing?" reply with depth, saying something like, "Well, I'm pretty scattered right now. I'm anxious about my kid's upcoming surgery, fatigued from lack of sleep, but pretty connected to my belief of hope." You'll energetically invite your colleague to also check in, and you'll find the dialogue that follows will reward both of you. It works.

Model Authenticity and Clear Often

Anyone on the team can step up to go first and model authenticity. True integration happens when it doesn't matter who goes first, because you all have embraced connecting. This will happen with practice. So, practice it every day in all interactions. Before the first month is out, everyone on the team will be able to lead and model the new rhythm.

For the first six months, we also recommend everyone bring at least one item to clear at the beginning of the meeting. These clearings will give the group confidence that they can successfully use the model.

Come Up with Unique Ways to Maintain Connection with Your Group

One way you can do this is to have each person offer up their own ice-breaker to use at the beginning of your meetings to help others get present. You could rotate responsibility around the group for a connective icebreaker. This helps everyone embrace the "responsibility" portion of ensuring that integration happens.

Remember that the heart of authenticity is connection. Creating impromptu social opportunities can help you and your colleagues remain close and aligned. If someone is going to a ball game, or happy hour, let the group know. Anyone that wants to attend can join. Whether they can attend or not is less important than the attempt to create a social connection. Feel free to involve your families in these events. The greatest way we get to know our coworkers is to connect with what is truly most important to them—their families. Annual cookouts or community service events are great ways to create those important connections with kids and spouses.

Take pictures of these events and post them around the office. Pictures always return us to special experiences.

You may also find group "apps" help you and your colleagues to share and stay connected. Sharing a quick note or a pic about the day's activities or something you are doing really helps the group stay connected with you.

Create a Culture of Recognition and Accountability

See if you can create a fun way to honor and recognize employees that are embracing the new normal. These culture champions are the types of ambassadors that we want to acknowledge.

You can also foster a culture that recognizes progress on the authenticity journey by establishing accountability assignments. These groups can identify different people to be responsible for the meeting agenda, offsite planning, and follow-up on tactical or strategic initiatives.

Schedule Offsite Events

We work with organizations to get their quarterly and annual offsite calendared. These become stake-in-the ground meetings that can't be missed and can only changed due to truly extreme circumstances (e.g., our house burned down! And you can only use that excuse once).

In addition to these specific actions, embracing the new speed limits that go with the authenticity journey can be a big step. If you are used to diving right into the meat of a meeting's agenda with full force, then slowing down the flow in the beginning can be difficult.

That's what the law firm partners used to do in their weekly case review session. They used to jump into the case docket, and most partners distracted themselves with their own details until they were involved in a particular matter (they "had been reading case and file updates to the wall" according to one partner). Now, after our second retreat with them, the partners had started using the anchor of checking in mentally, emotionally, physically, and spiritually as a way to slow down and get present at the beginning of the case review meeting. When we polled the partners three months later, we heard, "Wow, what a difference—I find myself relaxed and looking forward to what is going on outside my orbit because I come away with a piece of gold that I wasn't even looking for."

The law firm took our suggestion and started using the clearing process at its monthly partnership meetings. They inserted clearing on the agenda after check-ins so they wouldn't forget. At first, it was awkward. They told us that without our coaching them, it didn't quite work. We suggested they employ this prompt:

"Take a moment to look around the table and make eye contact with each partner. If you are triggered in that glance, take stock of your emotions, get a handle on the facts, and get back in alignment by preparing to clear with this partner."

The managing partner started reading this prompt from a cue card. It led to a flow of meaningful clearings that opened space for collaboration. After several meetings, he dropped the cue card and owned the prompt in his words.

We Know This Tune: The New Culture Emerges

The law firm got on track with regular meetings, and more importantly, found a rhythm that worked for its partners and associates. While we were waiting for the managing partner in a conference room, a senior associate dropped by and said that it was a miracle that the environment had been transformed from a difficult—and often cutthroat—place to one of collaboration. She shared that a spirit of camaraderie and teamwork had replaced the clear silos and divisiveness among the partners. She was in the department of trusts and estates (T&E) and had dreaded looking for support from the litigation department because of infighting between the two head partners of each department. The head of T&E had an about-face after a clearing at one of the regular meetings. The senior associate responded to the impact the clearings had on the office environment: "We used to keep our heads down in the afternoon after the partners' meetings, and now we actually look forward to it. We'll get an update and usually clever insight that help us immediately."

The impact of the authentic cultural revolution will yield a new way of being that sets up the team for success. Now this experience isn't a one-time event, it is standard operating procedure. The new rhythm isn't an annual retreat, but what you do day in and day out in your meetings and how you engage with each other.

The cadence and depth of your formal and spontaneous interactions will elevate each individual and team to new levels of growth and opportunity.

This way of connecting now is a result of your conscious choice to authentically connect. With practice, your default relationship will shift from working alone to collaborating together. You'll know that what may have previously seemed like more work is actually going to create more energy for individuals and teams.

These steps will help create safety for you and the team. This allows the catalyst to come from any person within the team. This can actually create a grassroots movement of the team that then brings the leader into the fold.

When we get to this point, employees become impatient and at times frustrated with superficial chitchat. The feeling that comes from a deeper level of operating is so compelling that it renders cliché the old norms from the past operating system. Everyone's radar is up to protect their new, incredibly valuable asset: an authentic culture.

To protect this asset, you may begin to hire people differently. Not only will they need the requisite technical or functional competencies, but they must be open and willing to participate fully in the new cultural norms. They must be aligned with the culture of transparency, open to learning how to remove the old-school business façade, and prepared to engage in a new way.

Visitors into your organization will feel the difference. There is a tangible difference between a team and a company that is deeply connected, aligned, and committed to one another and their organization, versus a team that silos around different responsibilities and has superficial interactions. The first environment is incredibly warm and welcoming, and people's intuitions will naturally pick up on this and yearning to understand what is so different about the place.

You can feel the difference.

CHAPTER 18

Real Journeys

. . . . . .

IT IS HARD to fully grasp the benefits that come with creating a culture of authenticity. The shifts and changes that come with that type of INpowerment are truly incredible. The best way we know to help you get a feel for the positive impact is to let real-life examples tell the story. Here are five different stories that illustrate what other organizations have experienced once they embraced authentic connection.

A Different Office

Thomas, founder and CEO of a growing retail chain of beauty salons, brought us in to help with their expansion. Their biggest challenge was recruiting and retaining talent. Or at least that's the way we framed it; Thomas referred to the problem as "putting bodies behind chairs." He had a white board in his office that had a running tally of bodies—he called it the "Body Count." His formula for success got him to 100 stores, but now his rate of growth was stalled. The team was running in place, and he was even having challenges retaining some of his top executives.

We brought his team on retreat for three days and worked on building safety for the team to (re)introduce themselves as the real people they were rather than as workers in the particular roles they played.

Joe was from Cincinnati. Sid grew up in Brooklyn. Cathy was the fourth generation in her family from New Jersey. Frank was originally from Toronto. Sarah was born in Israel and grew up in Miami; and Greg was from Salt Lake City. They shared their stories, owned and expressed their regrets, their triumphs and defeats, and even their aspirations and dreams. They bonded. They connected. Moreover, Thomas started to appreciate his team as people instead of as employees. He recognized the possibility that his office had lots of people with unique stories.

On the retreat's final night, Thomas revealed, "You guys taught me that there is more to our business than numbers or my Body Count. I have sold most of you short. I'm pretty sure I've underestimated the store managers and stylists back in our stores. They are far more than numbers. They are real people with heart in each of their stories. We need to shift the way we're going after growth. First, I want to stop the bleeding of attrition by recognizing our staff as people; and second, I want to change the way we go after new people."

This new sentiment spread once everyone returned to the office. Thomas continued to be relentless about the organization's growth possibilities, but his aspirations for those lofty goals were no longer just about him and his success—they now included his teammates and incorporated their stories. In the office, Thomas would boast about how Greg had a breakthrough idea about a new coloring service, or how Joe came up with a way to save on common area maintenance costs at mall locations. Throughout the head office and into the field, word spread about a new kind of energy.

When a "new office" experience emerges after authentic connection is established, it feels as though barriers have been lifted and power liberated.

Once you have successfully followed the process of building safety, like Thomas did, you have created a whole new way of interacting with each other in the daily rhythm of the office. You can appreciate that it's critical that you connect with each person as an individual distinct from the roles that they play within the organization.

Another Amazing Change in the Office

When Richard, the president and CEO of a regional automotive parts distributor, reached out to us, he was looking for a resource to lead his annual management offsite. His company had been doing offsite events for the past five years, and he needed someone to lead this one.

Although Richard was looking to deepen the team's trust and connections, he didn't have a burning objective outside of that. We told him we would go through our preparation process, with surveys and interviews of all the attendees, and then come back to him with a suggested agenda.

His company had been hit hard with the recession, but they had a reputation for having exceptional customer service. Although they didn't have the economies of scale that the larger national brands leveraged, their customers considered them a place they liked to bring their business. We had a feeling that a common theme would emerge, given all that they had been through.

We distributed questionnaires and then spoke with each person to get a very clear idea of what the group most needed so they could be more successful. The senior and regional management team, roughly sixteen people, began to open up. They had all been through the "war" of the recession and had little time to see the forest for the trees. They felt like they were on the other side, but weren't sure exactly where they were headed. It became clear to us that what they most needed was to create clarity and complete alignment around the mission and direction of the company, while deepening the trust and connection of everyone involved. The beautiful thing is that these objectives came from them. The CEO agreed and was completely on board.

One of the retreat's first exercises was to have everyone break out into four groups and identify the top five stories that exemplified what they might call "the best of the best" of what was special about this company. These stories could be about customers, situations with employees, and partnerships with vendors or investors.

Although there was some overlap in stories from group to group, we ended up with around fifteen different stories that time and time again showed how the CEO and the organization had gone "above and beyond" for one of their stakeholders. It was a poignant moment as the sense of pride, camaraderie, and awareness of how they had truly made a difference in people's lives dawned on everyone.

Armed with this clarity, we looked at the underlying purpose of their automotive parts organization. Although this exercise is always challenging for people trying to get the right words, the sentiment was consistent from the different groups. This whole notion of going above and beyond was clear. The purpose that ultimately fit for this organization was "Everyone deserves more!"

The beautiful part about this process is that this mission wasn't a marketing slogan that they needed to bring to life. They were simply naming what was already true before clarifying what their core purpose was for everyone—and then creating excitement and alignment around that belief.

We went on to look at a strategic direction and ultimately created a list of strategic and tactical initiatives for this group, as well as a new rhythm for coming together on a monthly basis to review progress and stay connected.

When we went back for the first monthly meeting, the office was buzzing. One of their first initiatives had been to capture the fifteen or so stories. They then asked all of the employees to submit other stories that were meaningful to them. After collecting all of these stories, everyone in the company was invited to read them to understand examples of their purpose that "everyone deserves more." The company also used these stories to help potential employees understand the culture and purpose of the company, and to ensure that new hires were ready to do what it took to live up to that purpose.

Additionally, the largest department had adopted the MEPS check-in process as a daily ritual with its entire team. It opened up doors of awareness and connection they'd never had before. It took about thirty or forty-five minutes every morning, but the department had never been tighter—and their performance was never better.

Speaking of performance, with the entire company focused on its core purpose, the company began to set monthly records for sales. This continued for eighteen straight months and ultimately provided the platform to take the company national.

Connect with Everyone's Humanity

Let's return to the story of the team members at our salon company client. Once they started seeing each other with a human (instead of purely commercial) lens, they worked with each other for change, growth, and opportunity.

Thomas, Joe, Cathy, Sid, Frank, Sarah, and Greg began to connect with the humanity of each other and with their other teammates in the office and stores. They developed a deeper level of understanding and respect for who they were as people, instead of just having a professional opinion of how everyone performed in their business roles.

For example, Sarah didn't just see Joe as the CFO. She now knew Joe as a guy who grew up in the Midwest and played sports throughout high school and college. She learned that Joe has four siblings, is divorced, and a single dad to three children under the age of ten. So now if Joe asked Sarah for a report she thought was a waste of time, she asked Joe why he needed it rather than rejecting him in a passive-aggressive way—her old way of dealing with him.

Throughout this whole company, role players were becoming seen as people playing roles, and people were helping others get more done more efficiently. From purchasing and real-time delivery of accessories to the stores, to sales and technical training, players became teammates and crossed the old, artificial barriers as they got stuff done.

The connection to each other's humanity not only created deeper appreciation and understanding among all of these players, it served as a bridge to increased productivity and profits.

Get Ready to Connect with YOUR Humanity

Most of us know the hard-charging, type-A leader that can be incredibly focused, hypercritical, and ultimately demanding about performance. There rarely seems a time when this person is actually enjoying their journey. They never show any emotion other than disdain for mediocre performance. They have more of a pit bull mentality; they are ready to strike and easily provoked into doing so.

This was the core issue when Jacob, the CEO of a regional app development firm, reached out to us. His leadership had completely devolved from a team into a siloed leadership group. It frustrated him to no end.

The problem was that Reena, the controller, had a reputation for being ferocious. She was highly respected for her business acumen and did a good job with the financial reporting. However, she was frequently compelled to step into every other functional department and call out the errors that she saw, even providing direction to those employees. Needless to say, her leadership team counterparts were not very happy with her.

We facilitated a leadership offsite. During our preparation interviews, each person on the leadership team commented that the problem was

Reena. If she would just stop "pissing in everybody's sandbox," everything would be okay.

These issues had been brought up before, though they were never properly cleared before the offsite. The controller was open to the clearings but unwavering in her challenge to the group that if anyone saw something they didn't like, it was their job to speak up! Ultimately the team was settling into a sense that her attitude would never change and that this friction was going to be constant. Because the company was still experiencing great results, they gave up on trying to be a full-fledged team and decided to remain in their silos to get things done, in spite of the friction that Reena brought to the team.

In the next exercise, we had the leaders step into the life-shaping experiences that created who they are, and everything changed. Each person's story, as you know for yourself, has challenges and difficulties. Rarely is there a dry eye as everyone begins to embrace their fellow teammates. This session was no exception.

Reena waited to go last. When she got up to share her experiences, she began by explaining in a very muted voice that she dreaded going through this exercise. You could see in her eyes that this was excruciatingly difficult. But, she persevered. She began describing the horrific journey she endured with her father dying from cancer and then her sister doing the same. It was a heart-wrenching story of loss. But it wasn't finished. She then told the team, for the first time, that she too was diagnosed with cancer ten years prior. It had come back five years ago, though now she was considered cancer free. Her ultimate takeaway was that she felt like her days were numbered. She didn't have time to wait to make her mark.

During this all, she was crying. All of her teammates were crying. We were crying too. Everyone now understood her humanity, the "why" behind her behavior.

As soon as she was done, Bart, the person on the team with whom she had the most contentious relationship with on the team, embraced her and told her what a courageous and inspiring person she was.

The tension in the air was gone. The only thing left was genuine care, understanding, respect, and commitment to support Reena and the team. They went from a team that wanted to vote Reena off the island, to a team that circled the wagons around her and embraced her sense of urgency to be outstanding—all because they connected with who she was as a person.

Seeing Hidden Power

Authentic connections illuminate hidden power that team members can now see in each other. Excited by the discoveries, they encourage each other to step into that power. Maybe now you understand why this connection is so powerful and why you were unknowingly yearning for this type of culture. You're grateful to see your vocational relationships expanding. It's life-giving for you and the team. It creates deeper meaning, respect, and fulfillment in your work. You are now open to sharing and receiving ideas and input.

When we last left Thomas and his beauty salon chain, Frank, the head of technology, saw the hidden power inside coworker Cathy with a broader perspective, and he wanted to coach, challenge, and support her in bringing that energy and talent to life. In the past, Frank would coast along in a meeting when Cathy presented merchandising ideas; he contributed what he thought he had to but never went beyond that baseline. During the retreat, however, Cathy and Frank connected and became kindred spirits when they discovered that they both lost siblings from tragic accidents during their childhoods. Since the retreat, they forged an authentic bond and started each day with coffee together. During a recent leadership and strategy meeting, Frank fully engaged and brought his "A" game to support Cathy when she pitched new merchandising campaigns. Moreover, he offered to observe and critique a dry run the evening before. Wanting her to win, he pushed her to see her own potential—beyond the limits she had put on herself. Cathy typically held back her most creative ideas. As Frank got to know the real Cathy, he caught onto the deep reserves she was hiding. Cathy, more comfortable after being vulnerable with Frank, expressed lack of self-esteem. Frank's authentic relationship with Cathy gave him permission to safely push Cathy to reach a new level of confidence fueled by his belief in her.

Finally I Can Let Go!

When Joe, a CEO from a regional food service distributor, called, he was looking for help developing his team. The business was doing well. He seemed to have a strong management team. This initially seemed like a scenario where things were good, but he wanted to make them better.

But in talking to Joe, we observed that he was completely stressed out. His anxiety was getting to him. He wasn't sleeping well. He wasn't eating properly. His doctors and wife were concerned with his weight. With some further conversation he admitted that he was afraid that he was drinking more as a coping mechanism and to help him sleep.

We were very curious as to why he was so stressed. What was driving this situation?

In our conversations with him, it became clear that, as the CEO, Joe felt he had to be the guy with all of the answers. It was his responsibility to provide direction to his team. He would drive the agenda each week at their management team meetings, and worked all weekend making sure he'd thought through all of the challenges and issues and had answers and directions for everyone on his team. No wonder he was so stressed and exhausted!

Maybe someone can do all that when they are a small company, but not if the business grows. His company was approaching $100 million, too big for him to continue operating it the way he had been.

So we did a corporate offsite with his management team of seven. Our goal was for him to be relieved of this burden of always having to have the answers. As we began to build the trust and connection of the team, its members began to share that they felt completely stifled. They felt like they didn't have any room to operate or feel like they could contribute to the direction of the company. In fact, several of them were looking for other opportunities.

It also came out that this burden wasn't coming from a place of ego or arrogance for Joe. Rather, it was a management style modeled to him by his father, who had started the business. So he was trying to honor the memory of his father by leading in the same way his father did.

By the second day, Joe let go and this pent-up desire to collaborate burst into the discussion. The synergy everyone felt was contagious. The entire team left feeling excited about the future. At the end of the meeting, Joe punctuated his "letting go" by saying "You all got this. I'm outta here!"

Then Joe left for a week of vacation—the first vacation he had taken in three years.

Feedback Loop

Not only are teams finding hidden power when they begin to connect authentically, they are also brave enough to share meaningful and con-structive feedback to avoid old pitfalls, traps, and artificial barriers. They are talking truth to build trust.

Our client Thomas, with the beauty salons, is now open to accepting the feedback he gets from his colleagues in a way that drives him to reach for and access his hidden power. Previously, he was dismissive of feedback as whining from ungrateful employees. Now, he appreciates feedback as a gift from partners who care about him (and his business). Sarah, the operations chief, is an expert in driving efficiency through people systems—she calls her specialty getting "return on effort." However, when she saw an opportunity to increase return on effort that was inconsistent with one of Thomas's pet peeves, she was not able to openly express her feedback to him. He intimidated her, and Sarah fell silent, losing her power.

Sarah has since practiced clearing with Thomas. It's awkward, yes, but it is becoming less scary for her. Not only is her newly expressed voice opening up her power, but Thomas has actively listened, seeing and appreciating her power and—more importantly—recognized that by accepting constructive feedback, he has the opportunity to grow his own power.

Can You Say Intervention?

Gary Jr. was completely frustrated. His company had a long-tenured, old-school-oriented, engineering-centric management team. There was no room for feelings or this touchy-feely crap. As the CEO of a family business, an international manufacturing firm that made extremely small sensors for other equipment, he needed his team to work together, especially given his key people were spread across three continents.

After two offsite events that had moved the dial with regards to trust and connection, the team reverted back to more of their same old methods. The team was so partitioned in their operations that they had little desire or use for connection and collaboration. Javier, their head of sales, openly confided in me that he didn't need the rest of the team for him to be successful. He was on autopilot and after twenty-five years with the company, was very comfortable doing things the way he had always done them. Tim, the COO with twenty-seven years at the company, was so busy with global operations that he didn't have time to worry about the others. They just needed to "do their jobs" and he would be happy. Almost to a person, they were banking on their long-standing relationships with Gary Sr., the original founder and patriarch of the company, to withstand any requests and new management philosophies from his son, the new CEO.

At this point, Gary Jr. was ready to clean house and bring in a whole new management team. As a precursor to his doing so, we talked him into letting us lead one more session, without him present, that delivered the message that if the team didn't "get it," he was going to dismantle and rebuild.

From our perspective, this became a team intervention. We wanted to help Gary's employees come out of denial to get the truth that their jobs depended on them changing their ways.

We structured this offsite with very clear boundaries and rules of engagement. We challenged everyone to take down their façades and show up authentically.

After a rough beginning, the chaos that was created from this information became a beautiful catalyst that led the team into deeper bonds and greater connection. People began opening up. And by the end of the two-day session, the looks around the room still had some healthy skepticism about how they were going to integrate these new processes, but they couldn't deny that they were the closest they had ever been as a team.

This closeness led to more open conversations, deeper levels of engagement in each other's challenges, and a growing sense of trust that the feedback process could be constructive. They each took ownership of following the new protocols and holding each other accountable to do the same. They realized that together, with these deeper level of conversations, they were opening the door to greater success as an organization.

Rally around Your Collective Power

Once you've connected with your colleagues authentically, team meetings are more productive: part pep rally, part think tank, and part war room. These cultural changes are working. The engagement from everyone has increased. So has their sense of contribution and fulfillment.

Role Modeling Paves the Way

When Richard, the CEO of a regional medical supply company that was undergoing a national expansion strategy, first called us, he was skeptical about how this type of process could really serve their company. He was dealing with major unrest within his current management team, and the expansion process was officially underway, meaning that the stress for the team would be growing. He knew that if the team didn't do something quick, they could come apart at the seams, significantly impacting the organization's short- and long-term goals.

Richard ultimately decided that making authentic connections would be worth the risk. During the first offsite, Richard had an opportunity to role model how to be more open and vulnerable with the team. He opened up with his personal story about growing up with an alcoholic, abusive father and a mother who was so terrified of her husband that she neglected the children to try to satisfy his father's every want and need. The tears were real. They fell naturally and endeared everyone in the room to this man. From that point forward, every person shared his or her stories vulnerably and openly, creating a depth of connection that they had never experienced before. This conflict resolution process (clearing) was easily adopted and utilized by the company afterward, because they were connected to each person and no longer taking things personally. They left the offsite aligned and connected, feeling like everyone had each other's backs.

Since that offsite, the national expansion of their organization has been going very smoothly. They have been on an acquisition tear, buying and integrating two to four companies each year. And about every four or six months, we will get a call from Richard, ready to do another offsite with his expanded group of new leaders from the acquisitions. He is a self-proclaimed student of personal development, but said he's still never experienced a more powerful event than the offsite retreats that we do with his team!

A Beautiful Closing

Finally, our leaders at the beauty salon company—Thomas, Joe, Cathy, Sid, Frank, Sarah, and Greg—have a greater sense of their collective power as a team. And they learned how to rally around that potential when they face a challenge, crisis, or opportunity.

A challenge in one department is no longer restricted to a silo where the problem needs to be fixed before word gets out that there is an issue. Instead, there is unrestricted freedom to share the burden of challenges to create opportunities for joint resolution—and occasionally solutions to those challenges emerge when multiple perspectives are invited in.

As an example, Sid noticed a drop in sales for one of their leading shampoo products and couldn't figure out the underlying cause. It had been the most popular and reliable seller, and with a handsome margin to boot. What was worse was that there was no substitute product that compensated for the shortfall. He was banging his head against the wall, and screaming at his assistant (who also was looking in the same place for the explanation), when he awakened to the idea that he could share the challenge with the leadership team. He realized that coming forward early was an act of vulnerability—a sign of courage, not weakness. Later, in the team exploration, they would discover the root cause, and hence the solution.

He assembled the team in an ad hoc session that evening and laid out all of the data. He admitted that he must have a blind spot because he was missing something. He asked for help. This admission inspired the collective power of the team to ignite, and the wealth of wisdom created an abundance of diverse ideas, perspectives, and ultimately clarity about the root cause that led to repackaging of the original product and a new spin-off product. Within four months, combined sales increased by over 30 percent. Sid invited the team to his home for a celebratory barbeque and attributed the success to the entire team.

When everyone is connected, victories—small and large—are no longer limited to one store, team, or department. Now, one team's victory is a win for the company. Each team member is on her or his feet ready to help and rooting for other team members who step up. What had been cutthroat has become collaborative. The collective power of the team is greater than any individual star.

CHAPTER 19

Wide Road Ahead: It's Your Brave New World

· · · · · ·

BY NOW, YOU are undoubtedly beginning to see the enormous possibilities for you and your team. But hopefully, you are starting to also imagine the potential beyond your conference room.

All IN!

By declaring that you are IN, you open a whole new way of approaching all the domains of your life—from the workplace to your home and your community. Most importantly, now that you're connected with the power of your personal leadership, you take responsibility for choosing how you bring your most precious gift—your presence—into the world.

This is your opportunity to take back your life. It's YOURS! You have one life to live. Your dreams and passions, your vision for what you want your life to be, requires this first step—to be all IN.

By taking this step you are saying to the world, "I am no longer a victim of my circumstances. I am responsible for my life." This INpowerment allows you to make choices differently every day in each aspect of your life. You get to answer all sorts of questions, intentionally and with your INpowerment: What is my attitude going to be today? Am I going to embrace gratitude in my life? Am I going to offer forgiveness to those who have wronged me so that I can let go of any resentment holding me back? Am I going to say "yes" to healthy relationships and "no" to toxic ones, even if the toxic ones have been around for a long time? Am I going to fight for what I'm passionate about? Am I going to fight for who and what I love? Am I going to do whatever it takes to be my best self today? Am I going to perform a random act of kindness today? Am I going to do the next right thing? Am I going to fight for the life that I want to live?

This holistic attitude can be prominently displayed in your work world as you have seen throughout this book. Imagine that you can use your workplace to create a safe environment for each team member to step up with their whole power and leverage your team as an incubator for personal learning and leadership development. Your new mantra could become: learn and practice at work, then bring your new insights to your family and community. This sort of growth is possible when you imagine it, set your intentions, and follow through together as a team.

Being IN Opens All Domains of Life

Once you are in touch with your authentic, internal power, everything changes! Wherever you go—to any domain: there you are, bringing your new INpowered self. When we speak of domains, those are the different areas of your life that are important to you, like your family, friends, self, vocation, faith, health, extended family, and community. What are the most important domains for you right now? Where do you want and need to focus your time and attention?

It is important that you bring your power into all of your domains, even when only one domain may be working for you now. We have heard of clients' marriages benefiting from the personal leadership transformation we seek in our offsite events. We have seen folks who'd been unfulfilled and merely going through the motions at the office become awakened to their own power in service work, and using it to make holistic shifts.

Stay attuned to when you are feeling authentic. Is it at work when your team is operating on all cylinders? If so, bring that spirit of connectivity home to the people you love. Or, are you connecting to the full power of your greatness when you come alive as a volunteer in a community group? If so, you also have the power to bring that authentic form of your personal leadership back to your home and to your work. Might your true connection to your authentic self be when you are IN your power as a parent? If so, take that to work. Even if you are not the boss, you can take the first step in creating authentic connections with members of your team. Take one small step.

One of the exciting processes we bring to leaders and teams is helping them create a life plan. How many of you have created a business plan? These plans are often how we continue to think about our business, which constantly challenges us to find that elusive ideal "work-life balance" where we are not so consumed by work that we have lost touch with our spouse, family, and the people that matter most to us. The problem is that when you are taking time away from work for family, then you get behind, so you take more time from family to catch up on work. This is the constant balancing act that we are trying to figure out but never seem to get right. To help achieve balance, we suggest investing as much time in your life plan as you do with business planning and forecasting. They are both important.

Unfortunately, trying to manage life balance with only a business plan starts with a win/lose scenario (either work wins and family loses or vice versa), and a zero-sum game where we must be involved seven days a week and twenty-four hours a day. This approach doesn't work.

A life plan, on the other hand, changes the nature of how we approach our lives. It's designed to help us be intentional with those key areas of our life that bring us joy and fulfillment. A life plan. Wow, what a novel idea!

Now that you are all IN for your life, a life plan becomes an essential component to help manifest what you most want in your life. By being intentional about what you want in each of your most important domains, you can focus on what you want to create. It helps you to capture the vision of what you want your life to be.

The key ingredient for a life plan is changing the win/lose scenario of a plan that only looks at our vocational life as multiple wins across all domains. Let's say you want to focus on your marriage, kids, health, leadership, and deepening your faith over the next year. Your life plan will allow you to create an intentional rhythm to connect to each of these five domains, inviting you to feel connected to the totality of your life in a real and meaningful way. This sense of accomplishment will increase your joy and fulfillment. That joy will be contagious in all of your domains! This means that even if you choose not to work over the weekend, the connection and fulfillment that you've experienced by being fully engaged in your life will translate into more creativity, energy, and enthusiasm when you are back at work. Because the energy from all areas of your life is connected, your "work" in your personal life helps you to be more effective at work, even though you are technically spending fewer hours.

This approach creates the most significant opportunity to manifest the life you want to live. Choosing to be all IN with your life allows you to choose what your life plan looks like based on your priorities and desires.

Maximize Fulfillment:
Purpose Makes the Difference

Now that you are choosing to be all IN for your life, you need to know your purpose, what drives you at your core. Your purpose provides you with the overarching guide for every choice you make. Aligning with your purpose is key to maximizing fulfillment in your life. It's what brings meaning to you.

Think about it this way. Just as every business has a mission statement designed to guide the company's focus, your purpose acts to give you focus for your life.

Purpose is always tied to your passions, what INspires you in your life. That is why you're here! When you connect to your passion, you can build it into your life plan so that you are intentionally embracing the best you can be in the world.

Knowing your purpose helps you be in alignment with your true power. It is an indescribable feeling that evokes the sweet spot where mental clarity, positive emotion, physical gratitude, and spiritual connectivity merge. And, as you authentically connect inside yourself, you immediately have the success formula for becoming the best leader, parent, sibling, child, and friend you can be.

All Together Now: Permission
Given for Everyone to Join You

Now that you are all IN within all your domains and you are aligned with your purpose and have stopped withholding your voice and actions, you will inspire others to do the same. They will see your passion and connect to who you are as an authentic person. When you are transparent and authentic, people can't help but connect with you. People will want what you have. They will see your self-acceptance and want the same.

People are desperate for genuine connection. It doesn't take that much to ignite the dormant, hidden, governed passions of others. Most people are aching for the key to unlock themselves from their self-imprisonment. But like Dorothy from *The Wizard of Oz*, they don't realize they have the power within themselves. You become the model for them to see themselves in a new light.

Your comfort with yourself will allow and compel them to be more themselves around you. Eventually, they will start to connect with their personal power differently. You are showing them, role modeling for them, what it means to be INpowered and authentic. They will start to own their thoughts and emotions differently, guiding them to make new and conscious choices about how to take responsibility for and change their lives.

And, it only gets better. When others around you are also connecting to their inside power, you are now all connecting to, with, and among each other in meaningful and powerful ways. The air is transformed wherever you are: the boardroom, the water cooler, and the living room. It is palpable. The value is created by the generative opportunity of multiple points of authentic connection that feed into, reflect off of, and continue to build upon each other like rays of light that become beacons into new possibilities.

Unlimited Possibilities

When people are stagnant and disconnected from their core, they disconnect from their own positive energy. They disconnect from the flow of what's in their hearts, which can only create feelings of negativity, guilt, shame, frustration, jealousy, and contempt. These negative emotions are likely to be repressed subconsciously so people can keep up the status quo.

Where does that negativity go? What happens to it? It is stored in our bodies. The brain captures and stores all of our emotions, and evidence is growing that the rest of your body stores those negative emotions as well, leading to physical ailments of high blood pressure, heart disease, addiction, depression, strokes, and cancer. Dr. Bessel Van der Kolk explains some of these discoveries in *The Body Keeps the Score: Brain, Mind, and Body in the Healing of Trauma*.[1]

But even more pernicious than what these stifled feelings do to you individually is how they leak out on others. Hurt people hurt people— many times unintentionally. A blow up with your spouse or an outburst at your kids often reflects these pockets of deep, stuck negative emotions. This negativity then extends from your family to the workplace where you may become withdrawn or isolated, shut down. Or maybe you go on the offensive and bully others. Ultimately the conflict shows up at work, and can then extend to your community as your coworkers are impacted by the negativity. Is it any wonder that we see so many social ills and issues in the daily news?

You can change that now.

The process to INpowerment creates an organic movement of positive energy that starts with you, then your team, and then gets distributed to your marriage, family, and community. Wherever you go, there you are, bringing this INpowered way of living. So the businesses, communities, cities, and countries that you engage with will be changed for the better. Each of these environments will unmistakably be impacted by this singular act that you bring when you authentically live your life.

You will bring a deeper sense of connection to others due to your deeper connection to yourself. The purpose that is yours to bring will touch the lives of those whom you come into contact with. Each of these people will be inexplicably moved, and they will move those with whom they interact. Thus you will co-create movement toward deeper levels of joy and fulfillment for everyone.

---

1   (New York: Viking, 2014). See also: http://www.health.harvard.edu/staying-healthy/anxiety_and_
physical_illness.

These movements culturally transform an organization, families, and communities. Each will be filled with new energy through the passions and gifts brought by INpowered individuals.

In order to change the culture that has so much negativity, we have to go back to each person and INpower them to connect to their positivity, their passion. And we have to INpower them to shed the limits on their inspiration, ideas, and creativity that connect to their passion. Let's create a movement of role models of authenticity—leaders and teams that are passionately changing the culture of their companies, families, and communities.

Businesses can embrace more than this quarter's earnings. They can simultaneously tackle global issues that before seemed unimaginable. At its core, this new way of operating, of being, is about moving from self- and group-limiting beliefs, to tapping into the infinite source of inspiration and abundance that create unlimited possibilities.

Great business teams enter new frontiers of opportunity as self-limiting beliefs give way to unlimited possibilities. Families connect at a deeper, more intimate and truthful way that begets legacies for future generations.

One person at a time, one company at a time, one community at a time—and the next thing you know, the world will become a better place for us all.

CHAPTER 20

Bring It to Work: Just the Tip of the Iceberg

• • • • • •

Challenges Revealed and Opportunities Pursued

THE VEIL IS lifted by authentic connection as sharing fosters a transparent environment where the team gets to the core issue and resolves it to free up energy to pursue the bigger opportunities.

When this happens, amazing changes begin to occur. Issues that were covered up will now be discussed, vetted, and resolved. Opportunities that were dormant or underachieved will now be targeted and pursued. Energy will fill the organization and overflow from the inside out—inside of every person, and out to the stakeholders and communities the organization serves. Each leader will feel INpowered to become their potential, paying huge dividends for the company and in all of the leader's life domains.

All issues become an opportunity to embrace the discomfort of sensitive conversations, which leads to the discovery that helps your team soar.

You become committed to this as a core value, to ensure that unspoken frustrations and fears don't snag you. You know what it's like to be limited by a lack of voice. So you and your team follow through to show up in an authentic way.

The potential is far reaching and joyfully imaginable. It's a magical shift from playing it safe to safely playing it. When the team "plays it safe," it avoids challenges and misses opportunities. Yet, when the team INpowers itself to "safely play," the team's authentic connections inspire emergence of enormous capacity. Game on!

From Lost to Leveraged

Power that was dormant or diminished is now embraced and leveraged. Once the new operating paradigm has been integrated, it becomes the foundation for even greater opportunities to maximize personal and team INpowerment.

This dormant or lost power is an untapped resource that you ultimately have control over. Instead of running on just four cylinders, run on all eight! By leveraging your full power, and the team's full power, you co-create synergy that elevates the entire team to a new level.

Power shifts from being lost, diffused, and diminished to channeled, embraced, and leveraged. Enormous power lies wasted in the recesses of each team member, under each work station, in the ether separating every person and cubicle, just waiting—waiting to be found from the lost, ready to be ignited into a cascading waterfall of creativity and spirited bounty of innovation. This is like the lost little boy and little girl inside, hiding until safe to come out.

Power held back diminishes the individual spirit and keeps out other team members from authentic connection to you. When you are INpower, you let team members see who you really are and know the best of you.

I'm Alive! Let's Take It on the Road

We can take this cultural movement and bring to communities, governments, nonprofits, and beyond. This is how you continue to show up more completely and fully in all the domains of your life, making it a lifestyle choice of how you show up in the world.

Once you catch on, it becomes viral. Get ready for the road show, because you will want to spread it to each person and every organization that matters to you. And, they will want IN because they are attracted to your POWER.

Map out your tour. Who will you visit first? Next? Close your eyes and imagine the reception. This is your time. You are alive and showing up with all you have. And you are igniting the nascent spark inside each of the souls along the path of your journey.

One Person DOES Make a Difference

Just as any one leader within a team can start the cultural transformation and bring change for self, team, and organization, the same is true in the other domains of your life. You can have an impact in your marriage, your family, your community—anywhere that a need for mutual respect and more authentic connection can infuse a new state of power.

We were working with Lonnie, who built a successful lighting distribution business that started in his garage and grew into a national organization with seven regional warehouses. He brought us in to help map out a succession strategy. It was difficult for Lonnie to let go of the idea of control, ownership, and the sense of meaning he derived from the business, yet he knew intellectually it was time to move forward. But there was resistance. Lonnie, someone who confidently and decisively built a lighting empire, was stuck.

And, then we dug deeper inside.

During one of our coaching sessions, he shared his regret that none of his children would succeed him. As we explored his sadness, Lonnie revealed that he was estranged from his kids following a painful divorce years earlier, and then immersed himself in growing the business. Crying deeply and longingly, he told us that he was responsible for his part in contributing to the estrangement, yet had held in his sadness and deep regrets for over 20 years. Ultimately, Lonnie recognized that he could take the first step to connect and engage with his children just by sharing his deepest truths—what he had just done with us. Remarkably, the next day he reached out and took the first step toward reconciliation, mutual understanding, and embracing the power of love that was locked up for decades. Lonnie, Jr.—who was in career transition at the time—joined the company as its successor, a happy ending that is recounted at family Thanksgiving.

This is the power of authenticity!

What have you been waiting for? Don't wait for someone else to start it. You are the one you've been waiting for. You've got exactly what you need to begin to make a difference—right here and right now. And, you will make a difference over there—at home, work, and in your community. The difference you make on just one other person may impact and inspire the next generation.

This Is REAL

No kidding, we've got real stories to back up the impact of the power of vulnerability. And, we can help you, too. This transformation has been achieved by organizations. And when organizations embrace this cultural norm and new operational modality, the results are incredible.

This hope isn't based on a theory or hypothesis from the book. It's based on our ACTUAL experience. Organizations we've worked with that have embraced this way of being have been transformed. Individuals who live by these principles are transformed. Essentially they are living their life connected to and emanating from their core. They are showing up as their best true self. We can attest to the impact that has on their families—and on our families. There is no question that we are better with those whom we care most about in the world because we have developed the capacity to authentically connect to ourselves and with them.

CHAPTER 21

There Is No Destination: The Journey Continues . . .

• • • • • •

Your Destination Is Here and Now

WITH PRESENCE AND power, you are right where you need to be right now—so, be INpowered.

Once you are, you will feel an ever-growing realization that you are aligned with yourself. This is a result of being in sync with your deepest truth. As you show up and realize you are where you are meant to be, that alignment will create an even deeper sense of purposefulness in how you show up.

It's not in the future or in the past. It's right here, with you, in this moment.

We find so many clients who wait for an event to occur before they take action. For example, we'll hear, "As soon as we onboard a new VP of Product Development, we'll commit to a team leadership offsite," or "Once we reach our next growth milestone, we'll start thinking about team development stuff." And so much opportunity ends up being lost when people postpone their transformations. Think about it this way: we are on a very long journey to a meaningful destination. And until then, we can simultaneously look ahead to where we're going while we focus on where we are right now.

Embrace the Journey to Authenticity

This is not easy. Change is never easy. But it does get easier as you continue to stay with our process.

Each successive challenge will make it easier for you to become comfortable being uncomfortable, with more elegance and greater impact. After all, you have spent all of your life becoming the way you are. Yet, now you can choose to become who you want—and are meant—to be. Set your intention and embrace the process outlined in this book to begin your next step. Get help when you need it. Invite your people to come with you on the road. When you get distracted, reembrace the process and get support. We are always ready and willing to help.

The Accelerator Is Accessible to All

Once you are IN, even though it started slow, the path to becoming truly connected actually goes faster. We call this process the accelerator—where we go slow to go even faster—and it is available to everyone. This is a completely inclusive model.

It takes some time to build a sense of safety. As we've said, this may feel like a slow-going process, but it sets the stage for having the ultimate accelerator in the future. Once that trust, connection, openness, and authenticity have been established, then it's time for warp speed. Real conversations happen in real time, with everyone around you. This is a simple truth, yet it's easily taken for granted—that the power to connect to ourselves and others is available to everyone, all the time, from your spouse and children to your team members and friends.

There are no limits or boundaries for connection except for the ones we make up. Reach out to anyone you see who is lost or whose power is diffused. Maybe initiate a conversation with your friend whose voice has been quieted by an unfortunate event. Include the teammate who you want to bet on because you believe from the data and your soul that she is a star on the verge of breaking out to shine.

INpowerment—the ability to create a safe place, where you can be yourself and have authentic connections—is a gift you have given yourself by reading this book. Now it's time to take it out to the world.

Life Doesn't Stop—Will You? Journey to a New Way of Being

Welcome to a universal language of connection without boundaries.

When we embrace the process of finding our authentic power and connection, we must acknowledge that there is no specific destination—there is only the journey. So this process becomes a lifetime of growth and expansion of your power and fulfillment. It only stops when you stop.

It's uplifting when you accept that your past is over but your future is just beginning. You are beginning the journey to a new way of being—a cultural revolution that transcends personal, family, corporate, and community domains. This transformation starts inside each of us as we accept and cultivate our inner power to connect with and influence others. Each team that embraces this power inspires the next team to join. Teams, families, and communities will discover new opportunities that were previously unimaginable.

The good news is that this journey and this power depend upon your choices. You are taking back your choice to live YOUR life and experience life to the fullest. Growing is a part of the process. Learning is the gift we get on the journey. Being a lifelong learner is a beautiful way to avoid complacency and stagnation. By shaking off the shackles of self-limiting beliefs, you have given yourself the ability to continue to find new ways to be INspired and to INspire others.

Isn't Life a Grand Adventure?
The Journey Continues

As soon as one cycle of growth concludes, another begins. This never-ending cycle can be an amazing adventure if we embrace all that it has to offer. The ups and downs are part of what we are meant to navigate and learn from, to grow from.

You are authentically connecting to your soul and inner wisdom. Inspired by that source, you create a way of being IN power with everyone who matters to you.

You have just one life to live—be ready each day to live it to its fullest.

The journey is right now, wherever you are. The challenge is right now—connecting to the power of your presence and connecting to the power of the presence of everyone in your immediate circle. Then, you will have co-created transformative power that you can bring into your mission and the world. The best part is that there are no limits. When you reach one destination, the journey continues onward . . .

ACKNOWLEDGMENTS

. . . . . .

Barry:

Thanks to June for believing in and encouraging me to ignite my passion and embrace my purpose, and for gifting me with a reminder of my power.

To Allie for her infinite curiosity about my work, which helped me bring stories to life by sharing them with her.

My abundant gratitude to Jeff for being a true partner, with whom I have shared this journey of ups and downs, and for ultimately helping to inspire me to overcome my own self-limiting beliefs about this project.

Jeff:

First and foremost, I thank my amazing sons, Chris Perez and CJ Manchester. They are the joy and inspiration for all that I do in my life. By far, the greatest gift in my life is the opportunity to be their Dad! I love you guys!

I also acknowledge the calling that this work represents in my life. Back in the mid-'90s I got a clear sense that my passion and direction for consulting needed to shift from technology to one supporting CEOs, presidents, leaders, and teams. This was where I was meant to focus my energies. I am truly blessed to be delivering this tremendously fulfilling work.

I also want to acknowledge my partner, Barry, for this amazing journey that we've been on together, both with Shift 180 and the writing of this book. It's not easy for two driven Type-A's to deliver work full-time to our clients, and then find time to write the chapters and then to create more time to collaborate on each chapter. It's been clear to both of us that this book is as much for us as it is for other leaders and teams. Throughout the journey of writing this book, our collaboration has continually complemented each other's ideas and created the synergy that we both have enjoyed.

Barry and Jeff:

We both are grateful to our editor, Chris Bengue, for encouraging and supporting us, and mostly, for understanding and committing to the purpose of our work. He has showed us how to bring that calling to the world as writers and story-tellers.

To our teacher, Cliff Barry, who taught and modeled for us the importance of creating a shame-free and safe container for teams. Thanks for being a mentor and friend.

We are also both eternally grateful to our YPO Forum for their unconditional love and support as our personal board of advisors for over 20 years. Their gifts of encouragement and feedback have been life-shaping and inspired our work and this book.

We have enormous gratitude to our clients who trust us with their sacred dreams and heartaches and courageously step into their power.

Index

ABOUT THE AUTHORS

· · · · · ·

BARRY KAPLAN, a partner in Shift 180, is respected as an expert in organizational development and leadership of people and teams, guided by his insight and compassion.

Barry has held entrepreneurial and senior executive roles in the tourism industry ranging from COO of a 200-store chain with over 2,000 employees; board member of a public company in the hotel, gaming, and restaurant business; president and board member of a public company in the dining and entertainment business; and, co-founder and senior executive of a twenty-one-company roll-up in the leisure travel business. Earlier in his career, Barry practiced corporate law.

Recognizing his signature strengths of identifying untapped potential in individuals and groups, coupled with decades of success in inspiring people and building teams, Barry chose to follow his passion and use his talents to guide leaders in their development as a full-time vocation. Barry is an executive and team coach for entrepreneurs, leaders, and their teams and actively leads small group, board, and management team offsites and retreats. Barry works extensively with YPO and EO, and has facilitated hundreds of forum retreats and training workshops.

Barry received his BS, *magna cum laude*, from the Wharton School, University of Pennsylvania, and a JD with honors from the George Washington University Law School. Passionate about cooking and hiking, Barry lives in New Jersey with his wife and daughter.

JEFF MANCHESTER has worked with over 1,000 presidents and CEOs as a strategic advisor, through one-on-one executive coaching, working with their management teams, in small groups and/or working with them and their spouses in couple's retreats. He is a master at INpowering individuals and teams to maximize their true potential through the gateway of authenticity.

Jeff brings to this work a lifetime of business management and consulting expertise, starting his career with one of the "Big 6" consulting firms, and then later, co-founding a highly successful systems consulting business. This business was recognized by *Inc.* magazine's "Fastest Growing 500 Companies" in 1992 and 1994.

As a serial entrepreneur, Jeff has engaged in different opportunities. He formed a brand management company focused on creating unique brands for elite professional athletes from Latin America. He was also one of the creators of the Latin Quarter Restaurant at Universal Studios' "City Walk" in Orlando, Florida, an award winner that continues to earn Best Latin Restaurant and Best Latin Night Club honors annually.

Jeff was and continues to be active member of YPO, serving as the past Chapter Chairman of the Florida Chapter. He is past network chair and current forum officer for the now YPO Miami-Ft. Lauderdale Gold Chapter and regional forum officer for the Southeast & Caribbean Region, and is the champion of the Cancer Focus Forum. He is also a member of the YPO Business Powered by Forum Taskforce.

Jeff holds an MBA from Florida State University. He also holds additional advanced degrees as a certified coach and certified group facilitator. He is a highly rated keynote speaker and certified forum facilitator, and trainer for YPO/WPO, for the last 20 years. He earned a bachelor's degree in business administration from Wittenberg University.

He is a proud dad to two amazing boys: his stepson, Chris, who was recently married, and his youngest son CJ, who is starting high school.